Mac OS X for Unix Geeks

Related Mac OS X Titles from O'Reilly

Essentials

AppleScript in a Nutshell
Building Cocoa Applications:
 A Step-by-Step Guide
Learning Carbon
Learning Cocoa with Objective-C
Mac OS X Pocket Guide
REALbasic: The Definitive Guide

Missing Manuals

AppleWorks 6: The Missing Manual
iMovie 2: The Missing Manual
iPhoto: The Missing Manual
Mac OS 9: The Missing Manual
Mac OS X: The Missing Manual
Office 2001 for Macintosh:
 The Missing Manual
Office X for Macintosh:
 The Missing Manual

Mac OS X Administration

Apache: The Definitive Guide
Essential System Administration
sendmail

Unix Essentials

Using csh & tcsh
Unix in a Nutshell
Unix Power Tools
Learning the bash Shell
Learning Unix for Mac OS X
Learning GNU Emacs
Learning the vi Editor

Related Programming

Developing Java Beans™
Java™ Cookbook
Java™ I/O
Java™ Network Programming
Java™ in a Nutshell
Java™ Swing
Learning Java™
Learning Perl
Managing and Using MySQL
MySQL Cookbook
Perl in a Nutshell
Practical C Programming
Programming with Qt

Mac OS X for Unix Geeks

Brian Jepson and Ernest E. Rothman

O'REILLY®

Beijing · Cambridge · Farnham · Köln · Paris · Sebastopol · Taipei · Tokyo

Mac OS X for Unix Geeks

by Brian Jepson and Ernest E. Rothman

Published by O'Reilly & Associates, Inc., 1005 Gravenstein Highway North,
Sebastopol, CA 95472.

O'Reilly & Associates books may be purchased for educational, business, or sales pro-
motional use. Online editions are also available for most titles (*safari.oreilly.com*). For
more information, contact our corporate/institutional sales department: (800) 998-9938
or *corporate@oreilly.com*.

Editor:	Chuck Toporek
Production Editor:	Claire Cloutier
Cover Designer:	Emma Colby
Interior Designer:	David Futato

Printing History:

October 2002:   First Edition.

ISBN: 0-596-00356-0
[M]   [12/02]

Table of Contents

Part I.   Getting Around

Part II. Building Applications

Part III. Beyond the User Space

Part IV. Appendixes

Preface

Once upon a time, Unix came with only a few standard utilities, and if you were lucky, it included a C compiler. When setting up a new Unix system, you'd have to crawl the Net looking for important software: Perl, *gcc*, *bison*, *flex*, *less*, Emacs, and other utilities and languages. That was a lot of software to download through a 28.8 kbps modem. These days, Unix distributions come with much more, and it seems like more and more users are gaining access to a wide-open pipe.

Free Linux distributions pack most of the GNU tools onto a CD-ROM, and now commercial Unix systems are catching up. IRIX includes a big selection of GNU utilities, Solaris comes with a companion CD of free software, and just about every flavor of Unix (including Mac OS X) now includes Perl. Mac OS X comes with many tools, most of which are open source and complement the tools associated with Unix.

This book serves as a bridge for Unix developers and system administrators who've been lured to Mac OS X because of its Unix roots. When you first launch the Terminal application, you'll find yourself at home in a Unix shell, but like Apple's credo—"Think Different"—you'll soon find yourself doing things a little differently. Some of the standard Unix utilities you've grown accustomed to may not be there, */etc/passwd* and */etc/group* have been supplanted with something called NetInfo, and when it comes to developing applications, you'll find that things like library linking and compiling have a few new twists to them.

Despite all the beauty of Mac OS X's Aqua interface, you'll find that a few things are different on the Unix side. But rest assured, they're easy to deal with if you know what to do. This book is your survival guide for taming the Unix side of Mac OS X.

Audience for This Book

This book is aimed at Unix developers, a category that includes programmers who switched to Linux from a non-Unix platform, web developers who spend most of their time in ~/public_html over an ssh connection, and experienced Unix hackers. In catering to such a broad audience, we chose to include some material that advanced users might consider basic. However, this choice makes the book accessible to all Unix programmers who switch to Mac OS X as their operating system of choice, whether they have been using Unix for one year or ten. If you are coming to Mac OS X with no Unix background, we suggest that you start with *Learning Unix for Mac OS X* (O'Reilly & Associates, Inc.) to get up to speed with the very basics.

Organization of This Book

This book is divided into four parts. Part I helps you map your current Unix knowledge to the world of Mac OS X. Part II discusses compiling, linking, and packaging applications, and Part III takes you into the world of the Darwin kernel and the X Window System. Part IV provides useful reference information.

Here's a brief overview of what's in the book:

Part I, *Getting Around*
> This part of the book orients you to Mac OS X's unique way of expressing its Unix personality.

> Chapter 1, *The Mac OS X Command Line*
>> This chapter will provide you with an overview of the Terminal application, including a discussion of the differences between the Terminal and your standard Unix *xterm*. The chapter also enumerates many of the available command-line utilities that come with Mac OS X.

> Chapter 2, *Startup*
>> This chapter describes the Mac OS X boot process, from when the Apple icon first appears on your display to when the system is up and running.

> Chapter 3, *Directory Services*
>> This chapter will get you started with Mac OS X's powerful system for Directory Services, which replaces or complements the standard Unix flat files in the */etc* directory.

Part II, *Building Applications*

Although Apple's C compiler is based on the GNU Compiler Collection (GCC), there are important differences between compiling and linking on Mac OS X and on other platforms. This part of the book describes these differences and explains how you can package applications for Mac OS X.

Chapter 4, *Compiling Source Code*

This chapter describes the peculiarities of the Apple C compiler, including using macros that are specific to Mac OS X, working with precompiled headers, and configuring a source tree for Mac OS X.

Chapter 5, *Libraries, Headers, and Frameworks*

Here we'll discuss building libraries, linking, and miscellaneous porting issues you may encounter with Mac OS X.

Chapter 6, *Creating and Installing Packages*

This chapter describes the native package formats used by Mac OS X, as well as some other packaging options you can use to distribute applications.

Part III, *Beyond the User Space*

This part of the book talks about the Darwin kernel, useful system administration tools, and setting up the X Window System to work alongside Aqua.

Chapter 7, *Building the Darwin Kernel*

Mac OS X is based on the open source Darwin kernel. This chapter describes how to download, compile, and install the source code for Darwin.

Chapter 8, *System Management Tools*

This chapter describes commands for monitoring system status and configuring the operating system.

Chapter 9, *The X Window System*

This chapter explains how to install the X Windows System and build X applications.

Part IV, *Appendixes*

The final part of the book includes miscellaneous reference information.

Appendix A, *The Mac OS X Filesystem*

Here you'll learn about the layout of the Mac OS X filesystem, with descriptions of key directories and files.

Appendix B, *Command-Line Tools: The Missing Manpages*

There are some great Mac OS X utilities that don't have manpages. This chapter provides them for you.

Developer Tools

This book assumes that you have installed the Mac OS X Developer Tools. If you bought the boxed version of Mac OS X 10.2 (Jaguar), the Developer Tools should be included on a separate CD-ROM. If you bought a new Macintosh that came with Mac OS X preinstalled, the Developer Tools installer will probably be in */Applications/Installers*. Failing either of those, or if you'd like to get the latest version of the tools, they are available to Apple Developer Connection (ADC) members at *http://connect.apple.com*.

Where to Go for More Information

Although this book will get you started with the Unix underpinnings of Mac OS X, there are many online resources that can help you get a better understanding of Unix for Mac OS X:

Apple's Open Source Mailing Lists
http://developer.apple.com/darwin/mail.html
    This site leads to all the Apple-hosted Darwin mailing lists, and includes links to list archives.

The Darwin Project
http://developer.apple.com/darwin/
    Darwin is a complete Unix operating system for *x*86 and PowerPC processors. Mac OS X is based on the Darwin project. Spend some time at this site to peek as deep under Mac OS X's hood as is possible.

Open Darwin
http://www.opendarwin.org/
    The Open Darwin project was founded in 2002 by Apple Computer and the Internet Software Consortium, Inc. (ISC). It is an independent project with a CVS repository that is separate from Apple's Darwin project, but it aims for full binary compatibility with Mac OS X.

Fink
http://fink.sourceforge.net/
    Fink is a collection of open source Unix software that has been ported to Mac OS X. It is based on the Debian package management system, and includes utilities to easily mix precompiled binaries and software built from source. Fink also includes a complete GNOME desktop distribution.

GNU-Darwin

http://gnu-darwin.sourceforge.net/

> Like Fink, GNU-Darwin brings many free Unix applications to Darwin and Mac OS X. GNU-Darwin uses the FreeBSD ports system, which automates source code and patch distribution, as well as compilation, installation, and resolution of dependencies.

Mac OS X Hints

http://www.macosxhints.com/

> Mac OS X Hints presents a collection of reader-contributed tips, along with commentary from people who have tried the tips. It includes an extensive array of Unix tips.

Stepwise

http://www.stepwise.com/

> Before Mac OS X, Stepwise was the definitive destination for OpenStep and WebObjects programmers. Now Stepwise provides news, articles, and tutorials for Cocoa and WebObjects programmers. Softrak (*http://softrak.stepwise.com/Softrak*) keeps track of software releases for Mac OS X, Mac OS X Server, OpenStep, WebObjects, and Darwin.

Conventions Used in This Book

The following typographical conventions are used in this book:

Italic

> Used to indicate new terms, URLs, filenames, file extensions, directories, commands and options, Unix utilities, and to highlight comments in examples. For example, a path in the filesystem will appear in the text as */Applications/Utilities*.

`Constant width`

> Used to show functions, variables, keys, attributes, the contents of files, or the output from commands.

`Constant width bold`

> Used in examples and tables to show commands or other text that should be typed literally by the user.

`Constant width italic`

> Used in examples and tables to show text that should be replaced with user-supplied values.

Menus/Navigation

Menus and their options are referred to in the text as File → Open, Edit → Copy, etc. Arrows will also be used to signify a navigation path when using window options; for example: System Preferences → Accounts → Users means that you would launch System Preferences, click the icon for the Accounts control panel, and select the Users pane within that panel.

Pathnames

Pathnames are used to show the location of a file or application in the filesystem. Directories (or *folders* for Mac and Windows users) are separated by a forward slash. For example, if you see something like, "...launch the Terminal application (*/Applications/Utilities*)" in the text, that means the Terminal application can be found in the Utilities subfolder of the Application folder.

%, #

The percent sign (%) is used in some examples to show the user prompt for the *tcsh* shell; the hash mark (#) is the prompt for the *root* user.

These icons signify a tip, suggestion, or a general note.

These icons indicate a warning or caution.

Comments and Questions

Please address comments and questions concerning this book to the publisher:

O'Reilly & Associates, Inc.
1005 Gravenstein Highway North
Sebastopol, CA 95472
(800) 998-9938 (in the U.S. or Canada)
(707) 829-0515 (international/local)
(707) 829-0104 (fax)

To comment or ask technical questions about this book, send email to:

bookquestions@oreilly.com

We have a web site for the book, where we'll list examples, errata, and any plans for future editions. The site also includes a link to a forum where you can discuss the book with the author and other readers. You can access this site at:

  http://www.oreilly.com/catalog/mosxgeeks/

For more information about books, conferences, Resource Centers, and the O'Reilly Network, see the O'Reilly web site at:

  http://www.oreilly.com

Acknowledgments for Brian Jepson

My thanks go out to Nathan Torkington, Rael Dornfest, and Chuck Toporek for helping me shape and launch this project, and to Ernie Rothman for joining in to make the book a reality. Also, thanks to Leon Towns-von Stauber for contributing Appendix B, *Command-Line Tools: The Missing Manpages*, to this book.

I'd especially like to thank my wife, Joan, and my stepsons, Seiji and Yeuhi, for their support and encouragement through my late night and weekend writing sessions, my zealous rants about the virtues of Mac OS X, and the slow but steady conversion of our household computers to Macintoshes.

I'd also like to acknowledge all the technical reviewers for this book:

- The folks at the ADC, for technical review and hand holding in so many tough spots.
- Erik Ray, for some early feedback and pointers to areas of library linking pain.
- Simon St. Laurent, for feedback on early drafts, and prodding me toward more Fink coverage.
- Chris Stone, for technical review and helpful comments on our Terminal.app coverage.
- Tim O'Reilly, for deep technical and editorial help.
- Brett McLaughlin, for lots of great technical comments as well as helpful editorial ones.
- Brian Aker, for detailed technical review and feedback on Unixy details.
- Chuck Toporek, for tech review and cracking the whip when I tried to let something lame slip by.

- Elaine Ashton and Jarkko Hietaniemi, for deeply detailed technical review, and some harsh but necessary comments that steered the book in a great direction.
- Steven Champeon, for detailed technical review and help on Open Firmware and the boot process.
- Simon Cozens, for technical review and pushing me toward including an example of how to build a Fink package.
- Wilfredo Sanchez, for an immense amount of detail on everything, and showing me the right way to do a startup script under Jaguar. His feedback touched nearly every aspect of the book, without which there would have been gaping holes and major errors.

Acknowledgments for Ernest E. Rothman

I would first like to thank Brian Jepson, who conceived the book and was generous enough to invite me to participate in its development. I would also like to express my gratitude to both Brian Jepson and Chuck Toporek for their encouragement, patience, stimulating discussions, and kindness. There are also many reviewers to whom I am grateful for useful suggestions and insights. I must also thank the visionary folks at Apple Computer for producing and constantly improving Mac OS X, as well as developers in the Mac OS X community who spend a great deal of their time writing applications and posting helpful insights on newsgroups, mailing lists, and web sites.

Finally, I wish to thank my lovely wife, Kim, for her love, patience, and encouragement and my Newfoundland dog, Samson (4/20/1991-4/19/2002), who was by my side during most of my efforts on this project but passed away before its completion. He will be forever in my heart.

## PART I

Getting Around

This part of the book orients you to Mac OS X's unique way of expressing its Unix personality. Chapters in this part include:

- Chapter 1, *The Mac OS X Command Line*
- Chapter 2, *Startup*
- Chapter 3, *Directory Services*

The Mac OS X Command Line

The Terminal application (*/Applications/Utilities*) is Mac OS X's graphical terminal emulator. Inside the Terminal, Unix users will find a familiar command-line environment. The first section of this chapter describes Terminal's capabilities and compares them to the corresponding *xterm* functionality when appropriate. The chapter concludes with a listing of the Unix tools that developers can find on Mac OS X.

Mac OS X Shells

Mac OS X comes with the TENEX C shell (*tcsh*) as the default user shell,* the Bourne-again shell (*bash*), and the Z shell (*zsh*). Both *bash* and *zsh* are *sh*-compatible. When *tcsh* is invoked through the *csh* link, it behaves much like *csh*. Similarly, */bin/sh* is a hard link to *bash*, which also reverts to traditional behavior when invoked through this link (see the *bash* manpage).

If you install additional shells, you should add them to */etc/shells*. To change the Terminal's default shell, see the "Customizing the Terminal" section, later in this chapter.

The Terminal and xterm Compared

There are several important differences between Mac OS X's Terminal application and the *xterm* common to Unix systems running X Windows:

- You cannot customize the characteristics of the Terminal with command-line switches such as *-fn*, *-fg*, and *-bg*. Instead, you must use the Terminal's Show Info dialog.

---

* */bin/csh* is hard-linked to *tcsh*.

- Unlike *xterm*, in which each window corresponds to a separate process, a single master process controls the Terminal. However, each shell session is run as a separate child process of the Terminal.

- The Terminal selection is not automatically put into the clipboard. Use ⌘-C to copy, ⌘-V to paste. Even before you press ⌘-C, the current text selection is contained in a selection called the pasteboard. The operations described in "The Services Menu" section, later in this chapter, use the pasteboard.

- The value of $TERM is vt100 when running under Terminal (it's set to xterm under *xterm* by default).

- Pressing PageUp or PageDown scrolls the Terminal window, rather than letting the running program handle it.

- On compatible systems (generally, a system with an ATI Radeon or NVidia GeForce AGP graphics adapter), the Mac OS X Terminal (and all of the Aqua user interface) will use Quartz Extreme acceleration to make everything faster and smoother.

If you need an *xterm*, you can have it; however, you will have to install a compatible version of the X Window System first. See Chapter 9 for more information about the X Window System.

Using the Terminal

The first order of business when exploring a new flavor of Unix is to find the command prompt. In Mac OS X, you won't find the command prompt in the Dock or on a Finder menu. The Terminal application is instead located in the */Applications/Utilities* directory. Don't open it just yet, though. First, drag the Terminal's application icon to the Dock so you'll have quick access to it when you need to use the Terminal. To launch the Terminal, click its icon in the Dock once, or double-click on its icon in the Finder view.

 The full path to the Terminal is */Applications/Utilities/ Terminal.app*, although the Finder hides the *.app* extension. *Terminal.app* is not a binary file. Instead, it's a Mac OS X *package*, which contains a collection of files, including the binary and support files. You can Control-click (or right-click) on the Terminal in the Finder and select Show Package Contents to see what's inside.

After the Terminal starts, you'll be greeted by the banner message from */etc/ motd* and a *tcsh* prompt, as shown in Figure 1-1.

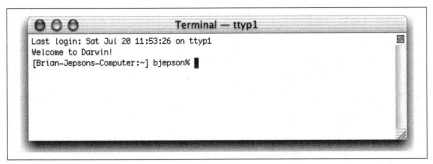

Figure 1-1. The Terminal window

Launching Terminals

One difference *xterm* users will notice is that there is no obvious way to launch a new Terminal window from the command line. For example, Mac OS X has no equivalent to the following commands:

```
xterm &
xterm -e -fg green -bg black -e pine -name pine -title pine &
```

Instead, you can create a new Terminal window by typing ⌘-N or selecting File → New Shell from the menu bar.

 To cycle between open Terminals, you can press ⌘-Right Arrow or ⌘-Left Arrow, use the Window menu, or Control-click on the Terminal's Dock icon to reveal a context menu of open Terminals. You can also jump to a particular Terminal window with ⌘-*number* (see the Window menu for a list of numbers).

You can customize startup options for new Terminal windows by creating *.term* and *.command* files.

.term files

You can launch a customized Terminal window from the command line by saving some prototypical Terminal settings to a *.term* file, then using the *open* command to launch the *.term* file (see "open" in the "Additional Shell Commands" section, later in this chapter). You should save the *.term* file someplace where you can find it later, such as *~/bin* or *~/Documents*. If you save it in *~/Library/Application Support/Terminal*, the *.term* file will show up in Terminal's File → Library menu.

To create a *.term* file, open a new Terminal window, and then open the Inspector (File → Show Info, or ⌘-I) and set the desired attributes, such as window size, fonts, and colors. When the Terminal's attributes have been set, save the Terminal session (File → Save, or ⌘-S) to a *.term* file (for example, *~/Documents/proto.term*). Now, any time you want to launch a Terminal window from the command line, you can issue the following command:

```
open ~/Documents/proto.term
```

 You can also double-click on *proto.term* in the Finder to launch a Terminal window. See "bindkey" under the "Additional Shell Commands" section, later in this chapter, for an example of binding a key sequence to this command.

The *.term* file is an XML property list (*plist*) that you can edit by hand or with the *Property List Editor* application (*/Developer/Applications*).* By default, opening the *.term* file creates a new Terminal window. You can configure the window so it executes a command by adding an execution `string` to the *.term* file. When you launch the Terminal, this string is echoed to standard output before it is executed. Example 1-1 shows an execution string that connects to a remote host via *ssh* and exits when you log out.

Example 1-1. An execution string to connect to a remote host

```
<key>ExecutionString</key>
<string>ssh xyzzy.oreilly.com; exit</string>
```

.command files

Adding the *.command* extension to any executable shell script will turn it into a double-clickable executable. The effect is similar to that of a *.term* file, except that you can't control the Terminal's characteristics in the same way. (A *.command* file will use the default Terminal settings.) However, you can stuff the shell script full of *osascript* commands to set the Terminal characteristics after it launches. An *osascript* is a shell command that lets you run AppleScript from the command line.† Example 1-2 is a shell script that sets the size and title of the Terminal, and then launches the *pico* editor.

---

* For more information on XML, see *Learning XML* (O'Reilly) or *XML in a Nutshell* (O'Reilly).

† To learn more about AppleScript, see *AppleScript in a Nutshell* (O'Reilly).

Example 1-2. Launching the pico editor

```
#!/bin/sh
# Script RunPico.command
osascript  <<EOF
tell app "Terminal"
  set number of rows of first window to 34
  set number of columns of first window to 96
  set custom title of first window to "PICO Editor"
end tell
EOF
pico $@
```

If you don't want to give the shell a *.command* extension, you could also use the Finder's Get Info option (File → Get Info, or ⌘-I) to choose which application will open with the executable. To do this, perform the following steps:

1. Highlight the script's icon in the Finder.
2. Choose Get Info from the File menu.
3. In the Get Info dialog, choose Open with:.
4. Click the drop-down menu and choose Other.
5. In the Choose Other Application dialog, select All Applications rather than Recommended Applications.
6. Find and choose the Terminal (*Applications/Utilities*) application.
7. Click Add.
8. Close the Get Info window (⌘-W).

As with any double-clickable application, you can assign a custom-made icon to your shell scripts and place them in the Dock. To change an icon, use the following procedure.

1. Copy the desired icon to the clipboard.
2. Select your script in the Finder and open the Get Info window (⌘-I). The file's icon appears in the upper-left corner.
3. Click the current icon, and use the Paste option (Edit → Paste, or ⌘-V) to paste the new icon over it.
4. Close the Get Info window (⌘-W) to save the icon to the application.
5. To add the shell script application to the Dock, locate the application in the Finder and drag its icon to the Dock.

Now you can click on the script's Dock icon to invoke the script.

Customizing the Terminal

To customize the shell used by the Terminal, start by changing the Terminal's Preferences (Terminal → Preferences). On the preference pane, you can tell Terminal to execute the default shell at startup or a specific command (such as an alternative shell).*

You can also adjust the Terminal's characteristics using Terminal → Window Settings (or ⌘-I), which brings up the Terminal Inspector, shown in Figure 1-2. Table 1-1 lists the available window settings. Changing these settings affects only the topmost Terminal window. If you want to change the default settings for all future Terminal windows, click the Use Settings As Defaults button at the bottom of the Terminal Inspector window.

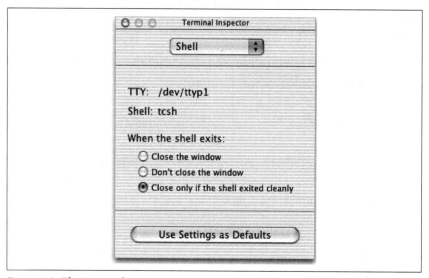

Figure 1-2. The Terminal Inspector

Table 1-1. Window settings

Pane	Description
Shell	Displays the shell used by the Terminal and lets you choose whether to close the Terminal window when the shell exits.
Processes	Displays the processes running under the frontmost window. You can also control whether Terminal will warn you if you try to close the window while you are running a program. You can disable this by choosing Never under "Prompt before closing window". You can also supply a list of commands that should be ignored, so if you're running a program (such as *vi* or *Emacs*) that's not in the list, the Terminal will warn you before closing the window.

---

* Although you can change the default shell in the Terminal preferences, this does not affect the login shell used for remote or console logins. See Chapter 3 for instructions on changing a user's default shell.

Table 1-1. Window settings (continued)

Pane	Description
Emulation	Controls the Terminal emulation properties.
Buffer	Sets the size and properties of the scrollback buffer.
Display	Changes the character set encoding, cursor style, font, and other attributes.
Color	Changes colors and transparency of the Terminal window.
Window	Controls window dimensions, title, and other settings.

One useful option available in the Emulation tab is "Option click to position cursor". If you enable this feature, you will be able to Option-click with the mouse to position the cursor in Terminal applications such as *vi* or *Emacs* (this could save you many keystrokes when you need to move the insertion point). This option also works over a remote login session, assuming that this is supported by the remote host's terminal capabilities.

Customizing the Terminal on the Fly

You can customize the Terminal in shell scripts using escape sequences or AppleScript commands. *xterm* users may be familiar with using the following to set the *xterm*'s title:

```
echo '^[]2;My-Window-Title^G'
```

Mac OS X's Terminal accepts this sequence as well.

 ^[is the ASCII ESC character, and ^G is the ASCII BEL character. (The BEL character is used to ring the terminal bell, but in this context, it terminates an escape sequence.) The escape sequences described here are ANSI escape sequences, which differ from the shell escape sequences described earlier. ANSI escape sequences are used to manipulate a Terminal window (such as by moving the cursor or setting the title). Shell escape sequences are used to tell the shell to treat a metacharacter, such as |, as a literal character rather than an instruction to pipe standard output somewhere else.

To type the ^[characters in *tcsh*, use the key sequence Control-V Escape (press Control-V and release, then press the Escape key). To type ^G, use Control-V Control-G. The *vi* editor supports the same key sequence; *Emacs* uses Control-Q instead of Control-V.

You can capture this escape sequence in a shell alias:

```
alias settitle 'echo -n "^[]2;\!*^G"'
```

Then you can change the title by issuing this command:

```
settitle your fancy title here
```

You may want to package this as a shell script and make it available to everyone who uses your system, as shown in Example 1-3.

Example 1-3. Setting the Terminal title in a shell script

```
#!/bin/sh
#
# Script settitle
# Usage:  settitle title
#
if [ $# == 0 ]; then
  echo "Usage:  settitle title"
else
  echo -n "^[]2;$1^G"
fi
```

You can also use *osascript* to execute AppleScript commands that accomplish the same thing:

```
osascript -e \
  'tell app "Terminal" to set custom title of first window to "Hello,
World"'
```

The Services Menu

Mac OS X's Services menu (Terminal → Services) exposes a collection of services that can work with the currently running application. In the case of the Terminal, the services operate on text that you have selected (the pasteboard). To use a service, select a region of text in the Terminal, and choose an operation from the Services menu. Mac OS X comes with several services, but third-party applications may install services of their own. When you use a service that requires a filename, you should select a fully qualified pathname, not just the filename, because the service does not know the shell's current working directory. (As far as the service is concerned, you are invoking it upon a string of text).

Here is a list of the services available in the Mac OS X Services menu:

Finder

The Finder services menu allows you to open a file (Finder → Open), show its enclosing directory (Finder → Reveal), or show its information (Finder → Show Info).

Mail

The Mail → Send To service allows you to compose a new message to an email address, once you have selected that address in the Terminal. You can also select a region of text and choose Mail → Send Selection to send a message containing the selected text.

Make New Sticky Note
> This service creates a new Sticky (*/Applications/Stickies*) containing the selected text.

Speech
> The Speech service is used to start speaking the selected text. (Use Speech → Stop Speaking to interrupt.)

Summarize
> This service condenses the selected text into a summary document. The summary service analyzes English text and makes it as small as possible while retaining the original meaning.

TextEdit
> The TextEdit service can open a filename, or open a new file containing the selected text.

View in JavaBrowser
> This service browses Java documentation for the selected class name. This is available whether the selected text is a real Java class name or not. (Garbage In, Garbage Out applies here.)

Using the tcsh Shell

The *tcsh* shell offers advanced command-line editing capabilities, filename completion, and a variety of customizations. Although *tcsh* is the default user shell, Mac OS X 10.2 (Jaguar) uses the Bourne shell (*/bin/sh*) for handling scripts (such as those found under the */etc* directory), and we suggest you do the same. However, *tcsh* is a fine user shell, and this section explains how to customize it and take advantage of some of its features.

Customizing the tcsh Shell

You can customize *tcsh* by changing certain environment variables, by creating aliases for frequently used commands, or by binding keys to commands (see "bindkey" in the "Additional Shell Commands" section, later in this chapter).

If you want to make your customizations permanent (so you don't have to issue the commands each time you log in), put the appropriate commands in one of *tcsh*'s startup files in your home directory. Here are some of the startup files into which you can put these commands:

.tcshrc
> This script is executed each time you launch a shell. When you open a Terminal window, *.tcshrc* is executed. If you start a sub-shell (or run a *csh* shell script), *.tcshrc* will again be executed. If your *.tcshrc* contains

recursive definitions, consider moving those commands to *.login*. For example, if you issue the command *set path = ($HOME/bin $path)* in your *.tcshrc*, then *$HOME/bin* will get prepended to your PATH environment variable each time you launch a sub-shell.

.login

This script is executed each time you launch a login shell, which includes opening a new Terminal window or logging in remotely. The *.login* script runs after *.tcshrc*. The *.login* file should contain settings that should only be applied once, such as PATH settings. The *.login* script is guaranteed to be run only once, regardless of how many sub-shells you invoke under a single login shell.

.logout

This script is run when you exit a login shell, but not when you exit a sub-shell.

The following listing shows what happens when you initially launch a shell, start a sub-shell, and exit the sub-shell and login shell:

```
Last login: Fri Jul 19 19:24:52 on ttyp1
Welcome to Darwin!
Running .tcshrc script
Running .login script
[Brian-Jepsons-Computer:~] bjepson% tcsh
Running .tcshrc script
[Brian-Jepsons-Computer:~] bjepson% exit
exit
[Brian-Jepsons-Computer:~] bjepson% exit
logout
Running .logout script
```

There are system-wide versions of these scripts, which are invoked before the scripts in a user's home directory: */etc/csh.login*, */etc/csh.cshrc*, and */etc/csh.logout*.

 tcsh will also read commands from the *.cshrc* fikle, if present, but if you have both a *.tcshrc* file and a *.cshrc* file, it will ignore *.cshrc*. For example, Fink (see Chapter 6) instructs you to insert a path in *.cshrc*, but if you've already got a *.tcshrc* file, that's where you should put the command instead.

Mac OS X borrows a handful of scripts from MIT's Project Athena to help simplify this configuration. On Mac OS X, sample *tcsh* configuration files are kept in the */usr/share/tcsh/examples* directory. In particular, this directory contains *.tcshrc*, *.login*, and *.logout* files named as *rc*, *login*, and *logout*. To use these configurations, create *.tcshrc*, *.login*, and *.logout* files that invoke the sample ones. This can be done by adding the following lines to your *.tcshrc*, *.login*, and *.logout* files:

```
source /usr/share/tcsh/examples/rc      # put this in ~/.tcshrc
source /usr/share/tcsh/examples/login   # put this in ~/.login
source /usr/share/tcsh/examples/logout  # put this in ~/.logout
```

Once this is done, you can then customize the *tcsh* environment by creating a *~/Library/init/tcsh* directory. You can create individual files in this directory for each type of customization.

aliases.mine
> Contains shell aliases.

completions.mine
> Contains command-line completions.

environment.mine
> Defines environment variables.

rc.mine
> Specifies run commands.

path
> Defines the command search path.

The startup scripts in */usr/share/tcsh/examples* will use these files, if they exist. Of course, you can simply use a *.tcshrc* file in your home directory. (The system-wide */etc/csh.cshrc* script will be read first.) For more information on *tcsh*, see *Using csh and tcsh* (O'Reilly).

Working with File and Directory Names

Traditionally, Unix users tend to avoid spaces in file and directory names, sometimes inserting hyphens and underscores where spaces are implied, as follows:

```
textFile.txt
text-file.txt
text_file.txt
```

However, most Mac users tend to insert spaces into their file and directory names, and in a lot of cases, these names tend to be long and descriptive. While this practice is okay if you're going to work in the GUI all the time, it creates a small hurdle to jump over when you're working on the command line. To get around these spaces, you have two choices: escape them, or quote the file or directory name.

To escape a space on the command line, simply insert a backslash (\) before the space or any other special characters, such as a parenthesis. Because they have meaning to the shell, special characters that must be escaped are: * # ` " ' \ $ | & ? ; ~ ( ) < > ! ^. Here is an example of how to use a backslash to escape a space character in a file or directory name:

```
cd ~/Documents/Editorial\ Reports
```

Or you can use quotation marks around the file or directory name that contains the space, as follows:

```
cd ~/Documents/"Editorial Reports"
```

There is one other way to get around this problem, but it involves using the Finder in combination with the Terminal application. To launch a Classic application such as Word 2001, which probably lives on the Mac OS 9 partition of your hard drive, you could enter the path as follows, using escape characters:

```
open -a /Volumes/Mac\ OS\ 9/Applications\ \(Mac\ OS\ 9\)/Microsoft\ Office\
    2001/Microsoft\ Word
```

Or you can enter the path using quotes:

```
open -a /Volumes/"Mac OS 9"/"Applications (Mac OS 9)"/"Microsoft Office
    2001"/"Microsoft Word"
```

As you can see, neither way is very pretty, and both require you to know a lot of detail about the path. Now for the easy way:

1. Type *open -a,* followed by a space on the command line (don't press Return yet).

2. Locate Microsoft Word in the Finder and then drag its icon to a Terminal window to insert the path after the space. When you do this, the spaces and any other special characters will be escaped with backslashes, as follows:

```
open -a /Volumes/Mac\ OS\ 9/Applications\ \(Mac\ OS\ 9\)/Microsoft\ Office\
    2001/
    Microsoft\ Word
```

3. Press Return to invoke the command and launch Word 2001. If Classic isn't already running, Classic will start, too.

You can also drag and drop URLs from a web browser, which can be used with *curl -O* to download files from the command line. For example:

1. Open a new Terminal window and type *curl -O* , with a space after the switch.

2. Bring up your web browser and navigate to *http://www.oreilly.com.*

3. Drag the image at the top of the page to the Terminal window. You should now see the following in the Terminal window:

```
curl -O http://www.oreilly.com/graphics_new/header_main.gif
```

4. Press Enter in the Terminal window to download *header_main.gif* to your computer.

Tab completion

If you want to type a long pathname, you can cut down on the number of keystrokes needed to type it by using tab completion. For example, to type */Library/StartupItems*, you could type */Li<tab>*, which gives you */Library/*. Next, type *S<tab>*. This time, instead of completing the path, you're given a choice of completions: *Screen Savers/Scripts/StartupItems/*. Type a little bit more of the desired item, followed by a tab, as in *t<tab>*. The full key sequence for */Library/StartupItems* is */Li<tab>St<tab>*.

If you have multiple completions where a space is involved, you can type a literal space with *\<space>*. So, to get a completion for */System Folder* (the Mac OS 9 system folder), you should use */Sy<tab>\<space><tab>*. It stops just before the space because */System* (the Mac OS X system folder) is a valid completion for the first three characters.

Command-Line Editing with tcsh

Mac OS X's default shell, *tcsh*, lets you move your cursor around in the command line, editing the line as you type. There are two main modes for editing the command line, based on the two most commonly used text editors, *Emacs* and *vi*. *Emacs* mode is the default; you can switch between the modes with the following commands:

```
bindkey -e    Select Emacs bindings
bindkey -v    Select vi bindings
```

The main difference between the *Emacs* and *vi* bindings is that the *Emacs* bindings are modeless (i.e., they always work). With the *vi* bindings, you must switch between insert and command modes; different commands are useful in each mode. Additionally:

- *Emacs* mode is simpler; *vi* mode allows finer control.
- *Emacs* mode allows you to yank cut text and set a mark; *vi* mode does not.
- The command-history-searching capabilities of the two modes differ.

Emacs mode

Table 1-2, Table 1-3, and Table 1-4 describe the various editing keystrokes available in *Emacs* mode.

Table 1-2. Cursor positioning commands (Emacs mode)

Command	Description
Control-B	Moves the cursor back (left) one character.
Control-F	Moves the cursor forward (right) one character.
Esc then B	Moves the cursor back one word.
Esc then F	Moves the cursor forward one word.
Control-A	Moves the cursor to the beginning of the line.
Control-E	Moves the cursor to the end of the line.

Table 1-3. Text deletion commands (Emacs mode)

Command	Description
Del or Control-H	Deletes the character to the left of the cursor.
Control-D	Deletes the character under the cursor.
Esc then D	Deletes the next word.
Esc then Delete or Esc then Control-H	Deletes the previous word.
Control-K	Deletes from the cursor to the end of the line.
Control-U	Deletes the entire line.
Control-W	Deletes everything to the left of the cursor.
Control-Y	Yanks the previously deleted string.

Table 1-4. Command control (Emacs mode)

Command	Description
Control-P	Recalls the previous command from history.
Control-N	Recalls the next command from history.
Up arrow	Recalls the previous command from history.
Down arrow	Recalls the next command from history.
File-fragment Tab	Performs command-line completion. *file-fragment* can be a filename, a directory, or an executable in your *$PATH*.
cmd-fragment Esc then P	Searches history for *cmd-fragment,* which must be the beginning of a command.
cmd-fragment Esc then N	Like Esc then P, but searches forward in the history.
Esc *num*	Repeats the next command *num* times.

vi mode

vi mode has two submodes, *insert* and *command* mode. The default mode is insert. You can toggle between the modes by pressing Esc. Alternatively, in command mode, typing **a** (append) or **i** (insert) will return you to insert mode.

Table 1-5 through Table 1-11 describe the editing keystrokes available in *vi* mode.

Table 1-5. Commands available (vi's insert and command mode)

Command	Description
Control-P	Recalls the previous command from history.
Control-N	Recalls the next command from history.
Up arrow	Recalls the previous command from history.
Down arrow	Recalls the next command from history.

Table 1-6. Editing commands (vi insert mode)

Command	Description
Control-B	Moves the cursor back (left) one character.
Control-F	Moves the cursor forward (right) one character.
Control-A	Moves the cursor to the beginning of the line.
Control-E	Moves the cursor to the end of the line.
Delete or Control-H	Deletes the character to the left of the cursor.
Control-W	Deletes the previous word.
Control-U	Deletes from the beginning of the line to the cursor.
Control-K	Deletes from the cursor to the end of the line.

Table 1-7. Cursor positioning commands (vi command mode)

Command	Description
h or Control-H	Moves the cursor back (left) one character.
l or Space	Moves the cursor forward (right) one word.
w	Moves the cursor forward (right) one word.
b	Moves the cursor back (left) one word.
e	Moves the cursor to the end of the next word.
W, B, E	Has the same effect as *w*, *b*, and *e*, but treats whitespace as a word separator instead of any non-alphanumeric character.
^ or Control-A	Moves the cursor to the beginning of the line (first non-whitespace character).
0	Moves the cursor to the beginning of the line.
$ or Control-E	Moves the cursor to the end of the line.

Table 1-8. Text insertion commands (vi command mode)

Command	Description
a	Appends new text after the cursor until Esc is pressed.
i	Inserts new text before the cursor until Esc is pressed.
A	Appends new text after the end of the line until Esc is pressed.
I	Inserts new text before the beginning of the line until Esc is pressed.

Table 1-9. Text deletion commands (vi command mode)

Command	Description
x	Deletes the character under the cursor.
X or Delete	Deletes the character to the left of the cursor.
d*m*	Deletes from the cursor to the end of motion command *m*.
D	Deletes from the cursor to the end of the line (similar to issuing d$).
Control-W	Deletes the previous word.
Control-U	Deletes from the beginning of the line up to the cursor.
Control-K	Deletes from the cursor to the end of the line.

Table 1-10. Text replacement commands (vi command mode)

Command	Description
c*m*	Changes the characters from the cursor to the end of motion command *m* until Esc is pressed.
C	Has the same effect as c$.
r*c*	Replaces the character under the cursor with the character *c*.
R	Replaces multiple characters until Esc is pressed.
s	Substitutes the character under the cursor with the characters typed until Esc is pressed.

Table 1-11. Character-seeking motion commands (vi command mode)

Command	Description
f*c*	Moves the cursor to the next instance of *c* in the line.
F*c*	Moves the cursor to the previous instance of *c* in the line.
t*c*	Moves the cursor just after the next instance of *c* in the line.
T*c*	Moves the cursor just after the previous instance of *c* in the line.
;	Repeats the previous *f* or *F* command.
,	Repeats the previous *f* or *F* command in the opposite direction.

Additional command-line keys

As we've just illustrated, the *tcsh* shell offers dozens of special keystroke characters for navigation on the command line. Table 1-12 lists some additional command-line keys for use in either *Emacs* or *vi* editing mode.

Table 1-12. Additional key commands for the tcsh shell

Key command	Description
Control-C	Interrupts the process; cancels the previous command (⌘-. works as well).
Control-D	Signals end-of-input for some programs and returns you to the shell prompt. If Control-D is issued at a shell prompt, it will terminate the shell session and close the Terminal window, if you've set your Terminal preferences to close the window when the shell exits.
Control-J	Has the same effect as pressing the Return (or Enter) key. Hitting Control-J after issuing a command will invoke the command, or it will take you to the next line in the shell if no command was given.
Control-K	Removes everything to the right of the insertion point.
Control-L	Clears the display.
Control-Q	Restarts the output after a pause by Control-S.
Control-S	Pauses the output from a program that's writing to the screen.
Control-T	Transposes the previous two characters.
Control-Z	Suspends a process. To restart the process, issue the *bg* or *fg* command to place the process in the background or foreground, respectively.
Esc then C	Capitalizes the word following the insertion point.
Esc then Esc	Completes the name if only a partial pathname or filename is entered.
Esc then L	Changes the next word to all lowercase letters.
Esc then U	Changes the next word to all uppercase letters.
Tab	Has the same effect as pressing the Esc key twice.

Additional Shell Commands

One of the first things that traditional Unix users will notice when they start poking around in the Terminal is that there are a few new commands they'll need to add to their repertoire. Two that we'll discuss here are *bindkey* and *open*. The *defaults* command is described in Chapter 8.

bindkey

Syntax

```
bindkey
bindkey [option]
bindkey [option] [key]
bindkey [option] [key] [command]
bindkey [option] [key] [string]
```

Description

bindkey is a *tcsh* shell command that is used to select, examine, and define key bindings for use in the Terminal.

Options

The following list describes the various uses of the *bindkey* command.

bindkey
> Lists all of the key bindings.

bindkey -c key cmd
> Binds *key* to the Unix command *cmd*.

bindkey -d
> Restores the default key bindings.

bindkey -e
> Changes the key bindings to *Emacs* mode.

bindkey key
> Lists the bindings for *key*.

bindkey key cmd
> Binds *key* to the editing command *cmd*.

bindkey -l
> Lists the editing commands and their meanings.

bindkey -r key
> Removes the binding for *key*.

bindkey -s key string
> Binds *key* to the string *string*.

bindkey -u
> Displays a message, showing how to use the *bindkey* command.

bindkey -v
> Changes the key bindings to *vi* mode.

For example, to create a binding between the F2 key and the *proto.term* script from the ".term files" section, earlier in this chapter, use this command:

```
bindkey -c ^[OQ 'open ~/Documents/proto.term'
```

To get the key sequence ^[OQ, type Control-V followed by the function key you want to bind, in this case F2. Now, any time you type F2 in the first Terminal window, it will open a new Terminal window using the settings saved in the *proto.term* file. You can put *bindkey* commands in your *.tcshrc* or *.login* script to make them permanent. For additional information on key bindings, and how to alter them, see *Using csh & tcsh* (O'Reilly).

---

open

Syntax

```
open file
open [-a application] file
open [-e] file
```

Description

The *open* command can be used to open files and directories, and to launch applications from the Terminal application.

Options

-a application
> Uses *application* to open the file.

-e file
> Forces the use of Mac OS X's TextEdit application to open the specified *file*.

Examples

To open a directory in the Finder, use *open,* followed by the name of the directory. For example, to open the current directory, type:

```
open .
```

To open your */Public* directory:

```
open ~/Public
```

To open the */Applications* directory:

```
open /Applications
```

To open an application, you need only its name. For example, you can open Project Builder (*/Developer/Applications*) with this command:

```
open -a "Project Builder"
```

 You are not required to enter the path for the application, only its name—even if it is a Classic application. The only time you are required to enter the path is if you have two different versions of applications with similar names on your system.

You can also supply a filename argument with the *-a* option, which would launch the application and open the specified file with that application. You can use this option to open a file with something other than the application with which it's associated. For example, to open an XML file in Project Builder instead of the default text editor, TextEdit, you could use the following command:

```
open -a "Project Builder" data.xml
```

To open multiple files, you can use wildcards:

```
open *.c
```

To force a file to be opened with TextEdit, use *-e*:

```
open -e *.c
```

The *-e* switch will only open files in the TextEdit application; it cannot be used to open a file in another text editor, such as BBEdit. If you want to use TextEdit on a file that is owned by an administrator (or *root*), *open -e* will not work. You'll need to specify the full executable path, as in:

```
% sudo /Applications/TextEdit.app/Contents/MacOSextEdit filename
```

Enabling the root User

By default, the Mac OS X *root* user account is disabled, so you have to use *sudo* to perform administrative tasks. Even the most advanced Mac OS X users should be able to get by with *sudo*, and we suggest that you do *not* enable the *root* user account. However, if you must enable the *root* user account, start NetInfo Manager (*/Applications/Utilities*), click the lock to authenticate yourself, and select Enable Root User from the Security menu.

Mac OS X's Unix Development Tools

The version of Unix that you'll encounter in Mac OS X's Terminal is similar to other versions you have seen, but dissimilar in some fundamental and often surprising ways. Although most tools are in their usual place, some are not on the system, while others are not where you would typically expect to find them on other Unix systems.

The lists shown in this section contain a sampling of the Unix commands developers will find on Mac OS X. It is, by no means, a complete list of the Unix utilities found on your system. Because there are so many commands, they are organized into several categories. If you are an experienced Unix user, many of these commands will be familiar to you, but we've referenced them here so you can quickly determine whether or not a command you need is available. Unless otherwise specified, all of the tools in the following lists can be found in */usr/bin* or */usr/libexec*. Some tools are available with the standard distribution of Mac OS X, but others are available only after installing the Developer Tools. (See Chapter 4 for more information about the Developer Tools). Appendix B contains a listing of commands that don't have manpages on Mac OS X.

Standard Unix Development Tools

The following commands are development tools that are commonly found on Unix and Linux systems.

bison
> A *yacc*-compatible parser generator.

cvs
> A high-level revision control system that sits on top of RCS.

flex, flex++
> A tool that generates lexical analyzers. See *lex & yacc* (O'Reilly).

---

cc, gcc
> Apple's customized version of *gcc*, the GNU C compiler.

gdb
> A source-level debugger.

gnumake, make
> Tools that automate the steps necessary to compile a source code package. See *Managing Projects with make* (O'Reilly).

rcs
> A command that manages file revisions.

unzip
> A tool that extracts files from a zip archive.

zip
> A command that creates a zip archive.

Apple's Command-line Developer Tools

The following list of utilities can be found in */Developer/Tools* after you have installed the Developer Tools package. Project Builder depends on some of these tools. Many of these tools have their roots in Macintosh Programmer's Workshop (MPW), Apple's old development environment.

agvtool
> Acts as a versioning tool for Project Builder projects.

BuildStrings
> Creates resource string definitions.

CpMac
> Serves as an alternative to *cp*; preserves resource forks when copying.

cvs-unwrap
> Extracts a tar file created by *cvs-wrap*.

cvs-wrap
> Combines a directory into a single *tar* file.

cvswrappers
> Checks an entire directory into CVS as a binary file.

DeRez
> Displays the contents of a resource fork.

GetFileInfo
> Displays extended information about a file, including creator code and file type.

lnresolve
> Returns the target of a symbolic link.

MergePef

Merges code fragments from one file into another.

MvMac

Serves as an alternative to *mv*; preserves resource forks when copying.

pbhelpindexer

Creates an index of Apple's API documentation for Project Builder.

pbprojectdump

Used by Project Builder's FileMerge feature to produce more readable diffs between file versions.

pbxcp

Supports Project Builder's build system; an internal tool.

pbxhmapdump

Debugs header maps; also internal to Project Builder.

ResMerger

Merges resource manager resource files. Project Builder's build system compiles *.r* files into *.rsrc* files using *Rez*, and if needed, Project Builder merges multiple files using *ResMerger*.

Rez

Compiles resource files.

RezWack

Embeds resource and data forks in a file.

sdp

Converts a scripting definition file into another format.

SetFile

Sets HFS+ file attributes.

SplitForks

Splits the resource fork, moving it from a dual-forked file into a file named *._pathname*.

UnRezWack

Removes resource and data forks from a file.

WSMakeStubs

Generates web service stubs from a WSDL file.

Also available in the */Developer/Tools* directory is a Perl script (*uninstall-devtools.pl*), which can be used to uninstall the Developer Tools.

Macintosh Tools

You can use the following tools to work with Macintosh files and disks, Macintosh applications, and the Macintosh clipboard.

bless
    Makes a system folder bootable.
diskutil
    Manipulates disks and volumes.
ditto
    Copies directories, and optionally includes resource forks for copied files.
hdiutil
    Manipulates disk images.
installer
    Installs packages; command-line tool.
lsbom
    Lists the contents of a Bill of Materials (bom) file, such as the *.bom* files deposited under */Library/Receipts*.
open
    Opens a file or directory. See "open" under the "Additional Shell Commands" section, earlier in this chapter.
pbcopy
    Copies standard input to the clipboard.
pbpaste
    Sends the contents of the clipboard to standard output.
screencapture
    Takes a screenshot of a window or the screen.
serversetup
    Configures network adapter properties. (Mac OS X Server only.)

Java Development Tools

You can use the following tools to develop, debug, and run Java applications.

appletviewer
    A Java applet viewer.
jar
    A Java archive tool.
java
    The Java Virtual Machine.
javac
    The Java compiler.

javadoc

A Java documentation generator.

javah

A tool that generates C and header files for JNI programming.

javap

A tool that disassembles class files and inspects member signatures.

jdb

The Java Debugger.

jikes

A fast open source Java compiler (installed as part of the Developer Tools package).

Text Editing and Processing

You can use the following tools to edit, convert, and otherwise manipulate text.

awk

A pattern-matching language for textual database files.

cut

A tool that selects columns for display.

emacs

GNU Emacs.

ex

A line editor underlying *vi*.

fmt

A tool that produces roughly uniform line length.

groff

A document formatting system that can render *troff* typesetting macros to PostScript, HTML, and other formats.

join

A tool that merges different columns into a database.

paste

A utility that merges columns or switches their order.

pico

A simple text editor designed for use with the Pine mailer. Note that the version of *pine* that ships with Mac OS X is much older than the current release.

sed

A stream editor.

texi2html
>A tool that converts Texinfo to HTML.

tr
>A command that substitutes or deletes characters.

vi
>A visual text editor.

Scripting and Shell Programming

The following commands include shells and programs useful in shell scripts.

echo
>A command that repeats command-line arguments on standard output.

expr
>A command that performs arithmetic and comparisons.

line
>A command that reads a line of input.

lockfile
>A command that makes sure that a file is accessed by only one script at a time.

perl
>The Practical Extraction and Report Language.

printf
>A command that formats and prints command-line arguments.

sh
>A standard Unix shell.

sleep
>A command that causes a pause during processing.

tclsh
>The Tool Command Language (Tcl) shell.

test
>A command that tests a condition.

xargs
>A command that reads arguments from standard input and passes them to a command.

zsh
>An enhanced Unix shell.

Working with Files and Directories

You can use the following tools to compare, copy, and examine files.

cat
> Concatenates and displays files.

cd
> Changes directory.

chflags
> Changes file flags.

chmod
> Changes access modes on files.

cmp
> Compares two files, byte by byte.

comm
> Compares two sorted files.

cp
> Copies files.

diff
> Compares two files, line by line.

diff3
> Compares three files.

file
> Determines a file's type.

head
> Shows the first few lines of a file.

less
> Serves as an enhanced alternative to *more*.

ln
> Creates symbolic or hard links.

 Symbolic and hard links are not the same as Carbon aliases that you create in the Finder (File → Make Alias). Unix programs cannot follow Carbon aliases, but all Mac OS X applications (Carbon, Cocoa, Classic, and Unix) can follow symbolic or hard links.

ls
> Lists files or directories.

mkdir
> Makes a new directory.

more
> Displays files one screen at a time.

mv
> Moves or renames files or directories.

patch
> Merges a set of changes into a file.

pwd
> Prints the working directory.

rcp
> Insecurely copies a file to or from a remote machine. Use *scp* instead.

rm
> Removes files.

rmdir
> Removes directories.

scp
> Secures alternative to *rcp*.

sdiff
> Compares two files, side-by-side and line-by-line.

split
> Splits files evenly.

tail
> Shows the last few lines of a file.

vis
> Displays nonprinting characters in a readable form.

unvis
> Restores the output of *vis* to its original form.

wc
> Counts lines, words, and characters.

zcmp
> Compares two compressed files, byte-by-byte.

zdiff
> Compare two compressed files, line-by-line.

File Compression and Storage

The following tools will compress, decompress, and archive files.

compress
> A tool that compresses files to free up space (use *gzip* instead).

cpio
> A utility that copies archives in or out.

gnutar
> The GNU version of *tar*; available only if you have installed the Developer Tools package.

gunzip
> A tool that uncompresses a file that was compressed with *gzip*.

gzcat
> A utility that displays contents of compressed files.

gzip
> A tool that compresses a file with Lempel-Ziv encoding.

tar
> A tape archive tool. GNU *tar* has more features and fewer limitations.

uncompress
> A utility that expands compressed (.Z) files.

zcat
> A tool that displays contents of compressed files.

Searching and Sorting

You can use the following tools to search and sort files.

egrep
> An extended version of *grep*.

fgrep
> A tool that searches files for literal words.

find
> A utility that searches the system for filenames.

grep
> A tool that searches files for text patterns.

locate
> A faster version of *find*; however, it depends on a database that is periodically updated by the weekly *cron* job in */etc/weekly*. If the database is out of date, *find* will be more accurate.

sort

A tool that sorts a file (use *-n* for numeric sorting, *-u* to eliminate duplicates).

strings

A tool that searches binary files for text patterns.

uniq

A utility that reports or filters duplicate lines in a file.

zgrep

A tool that searches compressed files for text patterns.

Miscellaneous Tools

The following tools will help you perform such tasks as searching the online documentation, switching user IDs, and controlling how programs run.

apropos

Locates commands by keyword.

clear

Clears the screen.

dc

Serves as a reverse-polish arbitrary precision calculator.

man

Gets information on a command.

nice

Changes a job's priority.

nohup

Keeps a job running even if you log out.

passwd

Changes your password.

script

Produces a transcript of your login session.

su

Allows you to become the superuser. Since the *root* account is disabled by default, you should use *sudo* instead.

sudo

Executes a command as another user. This tool is usually used to temporarily gain superuser privileges.

## CHAPTER 2

Startup

The most striking difference between Mac OS X and other flavors of Unix is in how Mac OS X handles the boot process. Gone are */etc/inittab*, */etc/init.d*, and */etc/rc.local* from traditional Unix systems. In their place is a BSD-like startup sequence sandwiched between a Mach* foundation and the Aqua user interface.

This chapter describes the Mac OS X startup sequence, beginning with the *BootX* loader and progressing to full multiuser mode, at which time the system is ready to accept logins from normal users. The chapter also covers custom startup items, network interface configuration, and Mac OS X's default *cron* jobs.

Booting Mac OS X

When the computer is powered up, the firmware is in complete control. After the firmware initializes the hardware, it hands off control to the *BootX* loader, which bootstraps the kernel. After a trip into Mach, the control bubbles up into the BSD subsystem, and eventually into the Aqua user interface.

By default, Mac OS X boots graphically. If you'd like to see console messages as you boot, hold down ⌘-V as you start the computer. To boot in single-user mode, hold down ⌘-S as you start the computer.

The BootX Loader

BootX is located in */System/Library/CoreServices*. It draws the Apple logo on the screen and proceeds to set up the kernel environment. *BootX* first looks for kernel extensions (drivers, also known as *kexts*) that are cached in the

---

* Mach is a microkernel operating system developed at Carnegie Mellon University. The Mac OS X kernel, *xnu*, is a hybrid of Mach and BSD.

mkext cache. If this cache does not exist, *BootX* loads only those extensions in */System/Library/Extensions* that have the *OSBundleRequired* key in their *Info.plist* file. Each extension lives in a folder (*ExtensionName.kext*), and the *Info.plist* file is an XML document that resides in its *Contents* subfolder. Example 2-1 is an excerpt from the */System/Library/Extensions/System.kext/ Contents/Info.plist* file.

Example 2-1. A portion of a kernel extension's Info.plist file

```
<?xml version="1.0" encoding="UTF-8"?>
<!DOCTYPE plist PUBLIC "-//Apple Computer//DTD PLIST 1.0//EN"
         "http://www.apple.com/DTDs/PropertyList-1.0.dtd">
<plist version="1.0">
  <dict>
    <key>CFBundleDevelopmentRegion</key>
    <string>English</string>
    <!-- multiple keys and strings omitted -->
  </dict>
</plist>
```

After the required drivers are loaded, *BootX* hands off control to the kernel (*/mach_kernel*).

Initialization

The kernel first initializes all the data structures needed to support Mach and BSD. Next, it initializes the I/O Kit, which connects the kernel with the set of extensions that correspond to the machine's hardware configuration. Then, the kernel finds and mounts the *root* filesystem. The kernel next loads *mach_init*, which starts Mach message handling. *mach_init* then launches the BSD *init* process. In keeping with Unix conventions, *init* is process ID (PID) 1, even though it was started second. *mach_init* is given PID 2, and its parent PID is set to 1 (*init*'s PID).

The rc Scripts

The *init* process launches the */etc/rc.boot* and */etc/rc* shell scripts to start the system. Both *rc* scripts (and all startup items) source the */etc/rc.common* script, which sets the initial environment, defines some useful functions, and loads the */etc/hostconfig* file. */etc/hostconfig* controls which system services need to be started and defines such things as the AppleTalk hostname. Example 2-2 is an excerpt from the *hostconfig* file.

Example 2-2. A portion of /etc/hostconfig

```
SSHSERVER=-YES-
WEBSERVER=-YES-
APPLETALK_HOSTNAME=*427269616e204a6570736f6ed57320436f6d7075746572*
```

This excerpt shows that *sshd* and *httpd* will be started on "Brian Jepson's Computer" (the decoded AppleTalk hostname) at startup. The AppleTalk hostname is encoded as a sequence of hexadecimal bytes (for example, 42=B, 72=r, 69=i, 61=a, and 6e=n).

After *rc.boot* has loaded in values from */etc/rc.common*, it determines whether the system is booting from a CD. Next, *rc.boot* tests to see whether the system is booting in single-user mode. If the system is neither in single-user mode nor booting from a CD, then *rc.boot* performs a check of the filesystem *(fsck)*. If the *fsck* fails, then *rc.boot* tries an *fsck -y*, which assumes a "Yes" answer to all the questions that *fsck* asks. If that fails, the system reboots (and may end up trying an *fsck -y* over and over again).

 If you find yourself in an *fsck* loop, you should boot from the Mac OS X installation CD. You can boot from a CD by holding down the C key at startup. When the Installer appears, choose Disk Utility from the Installer menu and use it to inspect and repair the damaged disk.

If *rc.boot* succeeds, *init* drops into a shell (for single-user mode) or launches */etc/rc* (for installation or multiuser mode). In single-user mode, only the *root* user may log in. In multiuser mode, the system is fully functional and ready to accept logins from normal users.

If */etc/rc* determines that the system is booting from a CD, it starts the Mac OS X installation program. (If you booted from a CD in single-user mode, you'll get dropped into a shell and */etc/rc* won't get run.) Otherwise, */etc/rc* mounts local filesystems and starts *kextd*, the kernel extension daemon. After that, it starts the Window Server and the *update* process (which flushes the filesystem buffers every 30 seconds). Finally, */etc/rc* enables the swap file, sets the language for the system, and hands off control to */sbin/SystemStarter*.

SystemStarter

SystemStarter examines */System/Library/StartupItems* and */Library/StartupItems* for applications that should be started at boot time. */Library/StartupItems* contains items for locally installed applications; you can also put your own custom startup items there. */System/Library/StartupItems* contains items for the system. You should not modify these or add your own items here. Table 2-1 lists Mac OS X's available startup items.

What Is kextd?

The kernel boots with the minimum set of extensions needed to mount the *root* filesystem on all supported hardware. Some of these extensions are not needed, so */etc/rc* starts the *kextd* daemon (*/usr/libexec/kextd*) to unload unnecessary extensions. For example, the *iPodDriver* includes the *OSBundleRequired* key to support booting from your iPod. If you don't have your iPod plugged in, *kextd* can safely unload that driver. The *kextd* daemon is also responsible for loading and unloading extensions for the duration of the system's uptime.

Table 2-1. Mac OS X default startup items

Item	Description
Accounting	Starts the *acct* daemon, which collects process accounting records.
Apache	Starts the Apache web server. Enable this with the WEBSERVER entry in */etc/hostconfig* or by turning on Web Sharing (System Preferences → Sharing).
AppServices	Starts the desktop database, input managers, and printing services.
AppleShare	Starts Apple file sharing. Enable this with the AFPSERVER entry in */etc/hostconfig* or by turning on File Sharing (System Preferences → Sharing).
AppleTalk	Starts the AppleTalk protocol. Enable this with the APPLETALK entry in */etc/hostconfig*.
AuthServer	Starts the authentication server. Enable this with the AUTHSERVER entry in */etc/hostconfig*.
BIND	Starts *named*, the Internet domain name server, if DNSSERVER is set to -YES- in */etc/hostconfig*.
ConfigServer	An empty startup script that maintains compatibility with earlier versions of Mac OS X, where this script was used to configure the network.
CoreGraphics	Starts the font and window server.
CrashReporter	Enables automatic crash report generation when an application crashes. Enable this with the CRASHREPORTER entry in */etc/hostconfig* or by selecting *Log crash information* in the Crashes panel of the Console application's Preferences (the Console application is located in */Applications/Utilities*).
Cron	Starts the *cron* daemon.
DirectoryServices	Starts *lookupd*, a daemon through which Directory Services is accessed.
Disks	Mounts local filesystems.
HeadlessStartup	Functions as a special startup routine used by headless servers, such as the XServe. Mac OS X Server only.

Table 2-1. Mac OS X default startup items (continued)

Item	Description
IPAliases	Sets up IP Aliasing (assigns multiple IP addresses to single physical adapter). Mac OS X Server only. Enable this with the IPALIASES entry in */etc/hostconfig*. See the *IPAliases(5)* manpage.
IPFailover	Starts a service that allows a server to take over for another server in case it fails. Mac OS X Server only.
IPServices	Starts *inetd* and, optionally, the *bootp* service.
LDAP	Starts *slapd*, the standalone LDAP daemon.
LoginWindow	Does nothing except to note the point at which the system is ready to display the login window. This is a placeholder service.
mDNSResponder	Starts the multicast DNS responder, which is used by Rendezvous for configuration.
MySQL	Functions as a startup script for MySQL. Mac OS X Server only. Enable this with the MYSQL entry in */etc/hostconfig*.
NFS	Starts the NFS client. The server is also started if NetInfo or */etc/exports* has been configured to export one or more filesystems.
NIS	Starts the Network Information Service unless NISDOMAIN is set to -NO- in */etc/hostconfig*.
NetInfo	Starts NetInfo. If the NETINFOSERVER entry is set to -YES- in */etc/hostconfig*, this will start up the *nibindd* daemon, which will start one or more NetInfo servers. If the entry is set to -AUTOMATIC- (the default), this will not start *nibindd* and will only start the local NetInfo server.
Network	Configures network interfaces and the hostname. If IPFORWARDING is enabled in */etc/hostconfig*, this script also enables IP forwarding.
NetworkExtensions	Loads various networking extensions.
NetworkTime	Starts the NTP client. Enable this with the TIMESYNC entry in */etc/hostconfig* or with System Preferences → Date & Time → Network Time.
Portmap	Starts the *portmap* daemon. Enable this with the RPCSERVER entry in */etc/hostconfig*.
PrintingServices	Starts the Common Unix Printing System (CUPS).
QuickTimeStreamingServer	Starts the QuickTime Streaming Server. Mac OS X Server only. Enable this with the QTSSERVER entry in */etc/hostconfig*.
SNMP	Starts *snmpd*, the SNMP daemon. Mac OS X Server only. Enable this with the SNMPSERVER entry in */etc/hostconfig*.
SSH	Starts *sshd*. Enable this with the SSHSERVER entry in */etc/hostconfig* or by enabling remote login in System Preferences → Sharing.
Samba	Starts the Samba service, which provides file services to Windows clients.
SecurityServer	Starts security services.
Sendmail	Starts *sendmail*. Enable this with the MAILSERVER entry in */etc/hostconfig*.
SerialTerminalSupport	Supports serial terminals for headless servers. Mac OS X Server only. See the *SerialTerminalSupport* script for configuration information.

Table 2-1. Mac OS X default startup items (continued)

Item	Description
ServerManagerDaemon	Starts the Server Manager daemon. Mac OS X Server only. Enable this with the SERVERMANAGERSERVER entry in */etc/hostconfig*.
SystemLog	Starts *syslogd*.
SystemTuning	Tunes the system based on details of your hardware configuration (such as the amount of installed memory).
VPN	Starts the VPN server. Mac OS X Server only. Enable this with the VPNSERVER entry in */etc/hostconfig*.
Watchdog	Starts the *watchdog* service, which monitors and restarts critical services when they quit unexpectedly. See the *watchdog(8)* manpage. Mac OS X Server only.

The Login Window

Once *SystemStarter* is finished, control is returned to *init*, which launches *getty*. In */etc/ttys*, the console entry launches the Login Window (*/System/ Library/CoreServices/loginwindow.app*). At this point, the system is fully functional and ready to accept logins.

Adding Startup Items

To automatically start applications, you have two choices: start them when a user logs in, or start them when the system boots up. On most Unix systems, startup applications either reside in the */etc/rc.local* script or the */etc/ init.d* directory. Under Mac OS 9, you could add a startup item by putting its alias in *System Folder:Startup Items*. Mac OS X has a different approach, described in the following sections.

Login Preferences

To start an application each time you log in, use the Login Items panel of System Preferences. This is good for user applications, such as Stickies or an instant messenger program. For system daemons, you should set up a directory in */Library/StartupItems*, as described in the next section.

Startup Items

If you compile and install a daemon, you'll probably want it to start at boot time. For example, MySQL will build out of the box on Mac OS X (you can download it from *http://www.mysql.com*).

A startup item is controlled by three things: a folder (such as *Library/StartupItems/MyItem*), a shell script with the same name as the directory (such as *MyItem*), and a property list named *StartupParameters.plist*. The shell script and the property list must appear at the top level of the startup item's folder. You can also create a *Resources* directory to hold localized resources, but this is not mandatory.

To set up the MySQL startup item, create the directory *Library/StartupItems/MySQL*. Then, create two files in that directory, the startup script *MySQL* and the property list *StartupParameters.plist*. The *MySQL* file should be an executable since it is a shell script. After you set up these two files as directed in the following sections, MySQL will be launched at each boot.

The startup script

The startup script should be a shell script with StartService( ), StopService( ), and RestartService( ) functions. The contents of */Library/StartupItems/MySQL/MySQL* are shown in Example 2-3. The function call at the bottom of the script invokes the RunService( ) function from *rc. common*, which in turn invokes StartService( ), StopService( ), or RestartService( ), depending on whether the script was invoked with an argument of *start*, *stop*, or *restart*.

Example 2-3. A MySQL startup script

```
#!/bin/sh

# Source common setup, including hostconfig.
#
. /etc/rc.common

StartService( )
{
    # Don't start unless MySQL is enabled in /etc/hostconfig
    if [ "${MYSQL:=-NO-}" = "-YES-" ]; then
        ConsoleMessage "Starting MySQL"
        /usr/local/mysql/bin/safe_mysqld --user=mysql &
    fi
}

StopService( )
{
    ConsoleMessage "Stopping MySQL"
    /usr/local/mysql/bin/mysqladmin shutdown
}

RestartService( )
{
    # Don't restart unless MySQL is enabled in /etc/hostconfig
```

Example 2-3. A MySQL startup script (continued)

```
if [ "${MYSQL:=-NO-}" = "-YES-" ]; then
    ConsoleMessage "Restarting MySQL"
    StopService
    StartService
else
    StopService
fi
}

RunService "$1"
```

 If you are using MySQL version 4 (in beta as of this writing), replace */usr/local/mysql/bin/safe_mysqld* with */usr/local/mysql/ bin/mysqld_safe*.

Because it consults the settings of the $MYSQL environment variable, the startup script won't do anything unless you've enabled MySQL in the */etc/ hostconfig* file. To do this, add the following line to */etc/hostconfig*:

```
MYSQL=-YES-
```

Mac OS X does not recognize any special connections between *hostconfig* entries and startup scripts. Instead, the startup script sources the */etc/rc. common* file, which in turn sources *hostconfig*. The directives in *hostconfig* are merely environment variables, and the startup script checks the value of the variables that control its behavior (in this case, $MYSQL).

You can manually start, stop, and restart MySQL by invoking this script from the command line:

```
/Library/StartupItems/MySQL/MySQL start
/Library/StartupItems/MySQL/MySQL restart
/Library/StartupItems/MySQL/MySQL stop
```

The property list

The property list can be in XML or NeXT format, and the list contains attributes that describe the item and determine its place in the startup sequence. The NeXT format uses NeXTSTEP-style property lists, as shown in Example 2-4.

Example 2-4. The MySQL startup parameters as a NeXT property list

```
{
  Description     = "MySQL";
  Provides        = ("MySQL");
  Requires        = ("Network");
  OrderPreference = "Late";
}
```

Over time, Apple will probably phase out legacy formats such as NeXT property lists, so it is best if you use XML property lists. The XML format adheres to the *PropertyList.dtd* Document Type Definition (DTD). You can use your favorite text editor or the *Property List Editor (/Developer/Applications)* to create your own property list. Example 2-5 shows the property list in XML.

Example 2-5. The MySQL startup parameters as an XML property list

```
<?xml version="1.0" encoding="UTF-8"?>
<!DOCTYPE plist
  SYSTEM "file://localhost/System/Library/DTDs/PropertyList.dtd">
<plist version="0.9">
<dict>
    <key>Description</key>
    <string>MySQL</string>
    <key>Provides</key>
    <array>
        <string>MySQL</string>
    </array>
    <key>Requires</key>
    <array>
        <string>Network</string>
    </array>
    <key>OrderPreference</key>
    <string>Late</string>
</dict>
</plist>
```

The following list describes the various keys you can use in a startup parameters property list.

Description
> This is a phrase that describes the item.

Provides
> This is an array of services that the item provides (for example, Apache provides *Web Server*). These services should be globally unique. In the event that *SystemStarter* finds two items that provide the same service, it will start the first one it finds.

Requires
> This is an array of services that the item depends on. It should correspond to another item's Provides attribute. If a required service cannot be started, the system won't start the item.

Uses
> This is similar to Requires, but it is a weaker association. If *SystemStarter* can find a matching service, it will start it. If it can't, the dependent item will still start.

OrderPreference

The Requires and Uses attributes imply a particular order, in that dependent items will be started after the services they depend on. You can specify First, Early, None (the default), Late, or Last here. *SystemStarter* will do its best to satisfy this preference, but dependency orders prevail.

Scheduling Tasks

Like other flavors of Unix, Mac OS X uses *cron* to schedule tasks for periodic execution. Each user's *cron* jobs are controlled by configuration files that you can edit with *crontab -e* (to list the contents of the file, use *crontab -l*).

Default cron Jobs

The global *crontab* file is contained in */etc/crontab*. It includes three *cron* jobs by default, which run the scripts contained in subdirectories of the */etc/ periodic* directory: */etc/periodic/daily*, */etc/periodic/weekly*, and */etc/periodic/ monthly*. Each of these directories contains one or more scripts:

```
/etc/periodic/daily/100.clean-logs
/etc/periodic/daily/500.daily
/etc/periodic/monthly/500.monthly
/etc/periodic/weekly/500.weekly
```

By default, */etc/crontab* runs them in the wee hours of the night:

```
15 3 * * *      root    periodic daily
30 4 * * 6      root    periodic weekly
30 5 1 * *      root    periodic monthly
```

So, if your Mac is not usually turned on at those times, you could either edit the *crontab* file or remember to run them periodically using the following syntax:

```
sudo periodic daily weekly monthly
```

As you'll see in Chapter 3, it is vitally important that you run these jobs to ensure that your local NetInfo database is backed up.

You should not modify these files, because they may be replaced by future system updates. Instead, create a */etc/daily.local*, */etc/weekly.local*, or */etc/ monthly.local* file to hold your site-specific cron jobs. The *cron* jobs are simply shell scripts that contain commands to be run as *root*. The local *cron* jobs are invoked at the end of the *500.daily*, *500.weekly*, and *500.monthly* scripts found in the */etc/periodic* subdirectory.

CHAPTER 3
Directory Services

A *directory service* manages information about users and resources, such as printers and servers. It can manage this information for anything from a single machine to an entire corporate network. The Directory Service architecture in Mac OS X is called Open Directory. Open Directory encompasses flat files (such as */etc/hosts*), NetInfo (the legacy directory service brought over from earlier versions of Mac OS X and NeXTSTEP), LDAPv3, and other services through third-party plug-ins.

This chapter describes how to perform common configuration tasks, such as adding a user or host on Mac OS X with the default configuration. If your system administrator has configured your Macintosh to consult an external directory server, some of these instructions may not work. If that's the case, you should ask your system administrator to make these kinds of changes anyhow!

Understanding Directory Services

In Mac OS X 10.1.*x* and earlier, the system was configured to consult the NetInfo database for all directory information. If you needed to do something simple, such as adding a host, you couldn't just add it to */etc/hosts* and be done with it. Instead, you had to use the NetInfo Manager (or NetInfo's command-line utilities) to add the host.

However, in Mac OS X 10.2 (Jaguar), NetInfo functions more as a legacy protocol. Instead of being a major player in the directory services world, NetInfo's role has been reduced to that of the local directory database for machines that are not participating in a network-wide directory, such as Active Directory or OpenLDAP. NetInfo is still present on Mac OS X systems, but you can perform most configuration tasks by editing the standard

Unix flat files. By default, Mac OS X 10.2 is configured to consult the local directory (also known as the NetInfo database) for authentication, which corresponds to */etc/passwd*[*] and */etc/group* on other Unix systems. You can override this setting with the Directory Access application. For more information, see "Configuring Directory Services," later in this chapter.

For users whose network configuration consists of an IP address, a default gateway, and some DNS addresses, this default configuration should be fine. You'll need to tap into Open Directory's features for more advanced configurations, such as determining how a user can log into a workstation and find their home directory, even when that directory is hosted on a shared server.

In order to work with Mac OS X's Directory Services, you must first understand the overall architecture, which is known as Open Directory. Directory Services is the part of Mac OS X (and the open source Darwin operating system) that implements this architecture. Figure 3-1 shows the relationship of Directory Services to the rest of the operating system. On the top, server processes, as well as the user's desktop and applications, act as clients to Directory Services, which delegates requests to a directory service plug-in (see the "Configuring Directory Services" section, later in this chapter, for a description of each plug-in).

Figure 3-1. The Directory Services architecture

Programming with Directory Services

As a programmer, you frequently need to deal with directory information, whether you realize it or not. Your application uses Directory Services each time it looks up a host entry, authenticates a password, or uses a printer. The Open Directory architecture unifies what used to be a random collection of flat files in */etc*. The good news is that the flat files still work. The other good news is that there is a brave new world just beyond those flat files. So, while all your old Unix code should work with the Open Directory architecture, you should look for new ways to accomplish old tasks, especially if you can continue writing portable code.

---

[*] */etc/master.passwd* is the shadow password file that actually contains the encrypted passwords.

To get at directory information, Unix applications typically go through the C library using such functions as gethostent( ). Higher-level APIs, such as Pluggable Authentication Modules (PAM) and Common Data Security Architecture (CDSA), also use the C library. Figure 3-2 shows how this works. The C library connects to *lookupd*, a thin shim that is the doorway to the *DirectoryService* daemon. The *DirectoryService* daemon consults the available plug-ins until it finds the one that can answer the directory query.

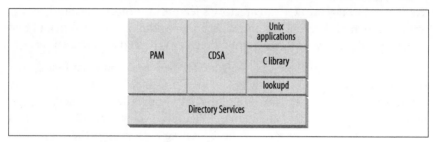

Figure 3-2. Accessing Directory Services

Working with Passwords

One possible route to user and password information is through the getpw* family of functions. However, those functions are not ideal for working with systems like Mac OS X that support multiple directories (flat files, NetInfo, LDAP, etc.). In particular, getpwnam( ) is not guaranteed to return a crypted password if the system has been configured to use another scheme, such as MD5 passwords. You should use the PAM API instead. PAM is included with, or available for, many flavors of Unix, so you can use it to write portable code. For more information on PAM, see the *pam(8)* manpage.

Configuring Directory Services

In order to configure Directory Services, use the Directory Access application (*/Application/Utilities*), shown in Figure 3-3. You can enable or disable various directory service plug-ins, or change their configuration.

Directory Access supports the following plug-ins:

AppleTalk
    This is the ultimate Mac OS legacy protocol. AppleTalk was the original networking protocol supported by Mac OS versions prior to Mac OS X. Linux and the server editions of Windows also support AppleTalk.

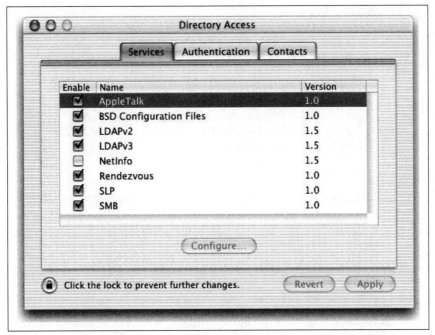

Figure 3-3. The Directory Access application shows the available plug-ins

BSD configuration files

These are flat files located in the */etc* directory, such as *hosts, exports,* and *services*.

By default, the checkboxes for NetInfo and BSD Configuration Files are off. For the BSD Configuration Files, the checkbox controls whether the files are consulted for Directory Service lookups. NetInfo is a little more complicated. If the checkbox is off, NetInfo uses the local domain but does not consult network-based NetInfo domains. If the checkbox is on, NetInfo will also look for and potentially use any network-based domains that it finds.

LDAPv2

This is a version of LDAP that Mac OS X can access (read-only).

LDAPv3

This is a newer version of LDAP, which Mac OS X fully supports (read-write). This is the same version of LDAP used by Microsoft's Active Directory and Novell's NDS. Mac OS X Server includes both the client and server components of OpenLDAP (*http://www.openldap.org*), an Open Source LDAPv3 implementation. The client version of Jaguar includes only the OpenLDAP client components.

NetInfo
This is a legacy Directory Services protocol introduced in NeXTSTEP.

 NetInfo and LDAP both use the same data store, which is contained in */var/db/netinfo/*. The data store is a collection of embedded database files.

Rendezvous
This is Apple's zero-configuration protocol for discovering file sharing, printers, and other network services. It uses a peer-to-peer approach to announce and discover services automatically as devices join a network.

SLP
This is the Service Location Protocol, which supports file and print services over IP.

SMB
This is the Server Message Block protocol, which is Microsoft's protocol for file and print services.

Under the Services tab, everything except NetInfo and BSD Configuration Files is enabled by default. However, if you go to the Authentication tab (Figure 3-4), you'll see that NetInfo is the sole service in charge of authentication (which is handled by */etc/passwd* and */etc/group* on other Unix systems).

By default, the Authentication tab is set to Automatic. You can set the Search popup to any of the following:

Automatic
This is the default, which searches (in order): the local NetInfo directory, a shared NetInfo domain, and a shared LDAPv3 domain.

Local directory
This searches only the local NetInfo directory.

Custom path
This allows you to use BSD flat files (*/etc/passwd* and */etc/group*). After you select Custom path from the pop up, click Add and select */BSD Configuration Files/Local*.

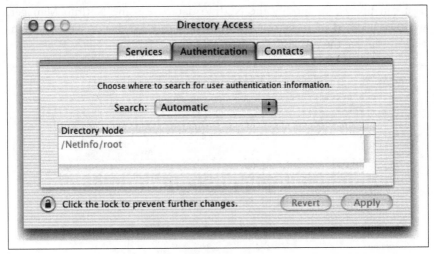

Figure 3-4. The Directory Access Authentication tab

After you have changed the Search setting, click Apply. The Contact tab is set up identically to the Authentication tab and is used by programs that search Directory Services for contact information (office locations, phone numbers, full names, etc.).

Note that enabling BSD flat files does not copy or change the information in the local directory (the NetInfo database). If you want to rely only on flat files, you would need to remove all the entries from the local directory and add them to */etc/master.passwd*. This would mean you could no longer use the GUI tools to manage those accounts.

NetInfo

The NetInfo directory is organized hierarchically, starting from the *root*, which, like a filesystem's *root*, is called /. However, this is not meant to suggest that there is a corresponding directory or file for each NetInfo entry. Instead, the NetInfo data is stored in a collection of files under */var/db/netinfo*.

You can browse or modify the NetInfo database using NetInfo Manager, which is located in */Applications/Utilities*. Figure 3-5 shows NetInfo Manager displaying the properties of the *mysql* user.

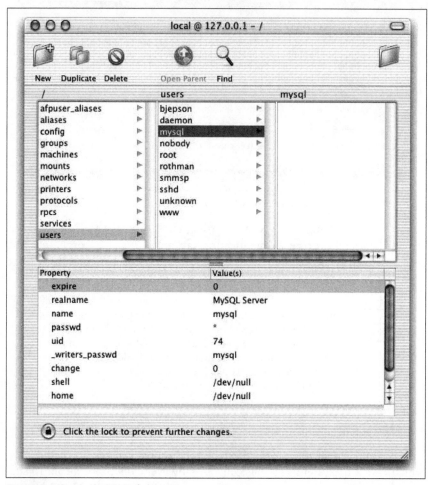

Figure 3-5. Browsing NetInfo

NetInfo Utilities

This chapter demonstrates four NetInfo utilities: *nicl*, *nireport*, *nidump*, and *niload*. Table 3-1 describes these and other NetInfo utilities.

Table 3-1. NetInfo tools

Tool	Description
nicl	Provides a command-line interface to NetInfo.
nidump	Extracts flat file format data (such as */etc/passwd*) from NetInfo.
nifind	Finds a NetInfo directory.
nigrep	Performs a regular expression search on NetInfo.
niload	Loads flat file format data (such as */etc/passwd*) into NetInfo.
nireport	Prints tables from NetInfo.

The *nidump* and *nireport* utilities display the contents of the NetInfo database. *niload* loads the contents of flat files—such as */etc/passwd* or */etc/hosts*—into NetInfo. *niutil* directly manipulates the NetInfo database; it's the command-line equivalent of NetInfo Manager. To modify the NetInfo database, use *sudo* with these commands or first log in as the *root* user. NetInfo commands that can be performed as a normal user are shown with the % prompt. If you need superuser privileges, the # prompt is shown. (Because the user can modify the shell prompt, be careful using this as a visual cue on a real system.)

Unlike other *ni** utilities, *nicl* acts directly on the database files. Consequently, you can use *nicl* to modify the local directory even when Directory Services is not running (such as when you boot into single-user mode).

When you use *niload*, *nicl*, or *niutil*, you are making potentially dangerous changes to your system. But even if you trash the NetInfo database with reckless usage of *niutil* and *niload*, you can restore the NetInfo database from your last backup. For more details, see the "Restoring the NetInfo Database" section, later in this chapter. To back up the local NetInfo database, use the command:

```
nidump -r / -t localhost/local > backup.nidump
```

NetInfo and Mac OS X Server

Mac OS X Server includes a graphical utility, Server Settings, shown in Figure 3-6, which handles the tasks described in this chapter.

Unfortunately, Mac OS X (the client version) does not include this utility, but the instructions in this chapter will help you accomplish the same things. You can also use the instructions in this chapter if you are connecting remotely through SSH to a Mac OS X Server.

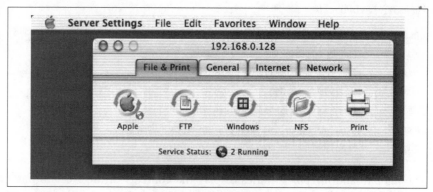

Figure 3-6. Mac OS X Server's Server Settings utility

NetInfo Command Reference

This section provides an overview of the NetInfo command-line utilities used in this chapter. The following sections, "Managing Groups" and "Managing Users and Passwords," demonstrate how to use *nicl*, *nireport*, *nidump*, and *niload*. For more details on these or other NetInfo utilities, see their respective manpages.

nidump

Syntax

```
nidump [-T timeout] (-r directory|format) [-t] domain
```

Description

You can dump NetInfo information in a flat file format (such as the */etc/hosts* format) or in a raw format that uses a C-like syntax:

```
{
    "name" = ( "localhost" );
    "ip_address" = ( "127.0.0.1" );
    "serves" = ( "./local" );
}
```

Options

-T timeout

   Specifies a timeout in seconds.

-t

   Treats the domain as a tagged domain, which includes a machine name and a tagged NetInfo database. For example, *abbot/local* refers to the local NetInfo domain of the machine named *abbot*.

-r directory
> Dumps the directory in raw format. Directory should be a path to a NetInfo directory, such as */users/root* or */machines.*

format
> Specifies a format corresponding to a Unix flat file of the same name. Can be one of: *aliases, bootptab, bootparams, ethers, exports, fstab, group, hosts, networks, passwd, printcap, protocols, resolv.conf, rpc, services,* or *mountmaps.*

domain
> Specifies a NetInfo domain. For standalone machines, use a dot (.), which refers to the local domain.

nireport

Syntax
> nireport [-T timeout] [-t] *domain directory* [*property* ...]

Description
You can list all NetInfo groups by using the *nireport* utility. To use *nireport*, use the following syntax:

Options
-T timeout
> Specifies a timeout in seconds.

-t
> Treats the domain as a tagged domain, which includes a machine name and a tagged NetInfo database.

domain
> Specifies a NetInfo domain.

directory
> Denotes a path to a NetInfo directory.

property ...
> Specifies one or more NetInfo properties. For example, each user listed in the */users* directory has *name, passwd, uid,* and *gid* properties (as well as a few other properties). Every directory has a *name* property that corresponds to the directory name. For example, the */machines* directory's *name* property is machines.

You can use *nireport* to list any portion of the NetInfo directory. For example, to list the top-level directory, specify the local domain, the / directory, and the *name* property, as in nireport . / name.

niload

Syntax

```
niload  [-v] [-T timeout] [(-d|-m)] [(-p|-P password)]
  [-u user] {-r directory|format} [-t] domain
```

Description

niload reads the Unix flat file format from standard input and loads it into the NetInfo database.

Options

-v

Selects verbose mode.

-T timeout

Specifies a timeout in seconds.

-d

Specifies that if a duplicate entry already exists, NetInfo deletes that entry before adding the new one. This can cause you to lose data if NetInfo is tracking information that isn't represented in the flat file. For example, if you dump the */users* directory to a flat *passwd* file format and load it back in with *niload -d*, you will lose the *picture*, *hint*, and *sharedDir* properties for every user on your system, because the *passwd* file does not have a field for those properties. Most of the time, the *-m* option is what you want.

-m

Specifies that if a duplicate entry already exists, *niload* will merge the changes. So, if you dump the */users* directory to a flat *passwd* file format, change a user's shell, and load that file back in with *niload*, NetInfo will keep the old shell. If you use the *-m* option, NetInfo will accept the new shell without the destructive side effects of the *-d* option.

-p

Prompt for a password. You can use this instead of prefixing the command with *sudo*.

-P password

Use the specified password.

 If your shell history file is enabled, the *-P* option presents a security risk, since the password will be stored, along with the history of other shell commands. It is best to avoid using this option.

-u user

Use the specified user's identity when running the command. You'll be prompted for a password.

-t

Treats the domain as a tagged domain, which includes a machine name and a tagged NetInfo database.

domain

Specifies a NetInfo domain.

directory

Denotes a path to a NetInfo directory.

format

Specifies a format corresponding to a Unix flat file of the same name. Can be one of the following: *aliases, bootptab, bootparams, exports, fstab, group, hosts, networks, passwd, printcap, protocols, rpc,* or *services.*

---

nicl

Syntax

```
nicl [options] datasource [command]
```

Description

Use *nicl* to modify entries in the NetInfo database. You can manipulate directories and properties with *nicl*. The *datasource* may be the path to a NetInfo directory (such as /) or the filesystem path of a NetInfo database (you must use the *-raw* option for this). Use *-raw* to work directly with the NetInfo database, such as */var/db/netinfo/local.nidb*. This is useful in cases when the NetInfo daemon is down (such as when you boot into single-user mode).

Options

-c

Create a new data source.

-p

Prompt for a password. You can use this instead of prefixing the command with *sudo*.

-P password

Use the specified password.

-q

Be quiet.

-raw

Indicates that the *datasource* is a filesystem path to a NetInfo database.

-ro

Open *datasource* as read-only.

-t

Treats the domain as a tagged domain, which includes a machine name and a tagged NetInfo database.

-u user

Use the specified user's identity when running the command. You'll be prompted for a password.

-v

Be verbose.

-x500

Use X.500 names (see the *nicl* manpage for more details).

Commands

-append path key val ...

Appends a value to an existing property. The property is created if it does not already exist.

-copy path newparent

Copies the specified *path* to a new parent path.

-create path [key [val ...]]

Creates a NetInfo directory specified by *path*. See the "Creating a User with nicl" section, later in this chapter, for a complete example.

-delete path [key [val ...]]

Destroys the specified path and all its contents. If you specify a key and/or value, only the specified key is deleted. For an example, see the "Deleting a Group" section, later in this chapter.

-domainname

Prints the NetInfo domain name of *datasource*.

-flush

Flushes the directory cache.

-insert path key val index

Operates like *-append*, but instead of placing the value at the end, it inserts it at the specified index.

-list path [key ...]

Lists all the NetInfo directories in the specified path. For example, to list all users, use *nicl / -list /users*.

-merge path key val ...

Operates like *-append*, but if the value already exists, it is not duplicated. See the "Adding Users to a Group" section, later in this chapter.

-move path newparent

Moves the specified *path* to a new parent path.

-read path [key ...]

Displays all the properties of the specified path. For example, to see *root*'s properties, use *nicl / -read /users/root*.

-search arguments

Performs a search within the NetInfo database. For complete details, see the *nicl* manpage.

-rename path oldkey newkey
 Renames a property.
-resync
 Resynchronizes NetInfo.
-rparent
 Prints the NetInfo parent of *datasource*.
-statistics
 Displays NetInfo server statistics.

Managing Groups

NetInfo stores information about groups in its */groups* directory. This is different from the */etc/group* file, which is consulted only in single-user mode.

To list all of the group IDs (GIDs) and group names for the local domain, invoke *nireport* with the NetInfo domain (., the local domain), the directory (*/groups*), and the properties you want to inspect—in this case, *gid* and *name*:

```
% nireport . /groups gid name
-2      nobody
-1      nogroup
0       wheel
1       daemon
2       kmem
3       sys
4       tty
5       operator
6       mail
7       bin
20      staff
25      smmsp
31      guest
45      utmp
66      uucp
68      dialer
69      network
70      www
74      mysql
75      sshd
80      admin
99      unknown
```

 Although the flat file format is called *group* (after the */etc/group* file), the NetInfo group directory is */groups*. If you forget that last *s*, NetInfo will look for the wrong directory.

Creating a Group with niload

The *niload* utility can be used to read the flat file format used by */etc/group* (name:password:gid:members). To add a new group, you can create a file that adheres to that format, and load it with *niload*. For ad hoc work, you can use a here document rather than a separate file:

```
# niload group . <<EOF
? writers:*:1001:
? EOF
```

Here Documents

A here document is a shell quoting syntax that allows you to send data to standard input as though it had come in from a file. You can use this syntax interactively from the command line or in a shell script. The EOF tag, shown in the previous example, can be any text string. The here document starts with <<STRING and ends when STRING appears on a line by itself. For example, you can sort a bunch of words with here documents. (The ? character is supplied by the shell to let you know it is expecting input.)

```
% sort <<WORDS
? gamma
? beta
? alpha
? omega
? WORDS
alpha
beta
gamma
omega
```

Creating a Group with nicl

To create a group with *nicl*, you'll need to create a directory under */groups* and set the *gid* and *passwd* properties. If you want a password, it must be encrypted with crypt( ). If you don't want a group password, use an asterisk instead. (Be sure to quote the * so that the shell does not attempt to expand it.) The following creates a group named *writers* as GID 5005 with no password and no members:

```
# nicl / create /groups/writers gid 5005
# nicl / create /groups/writers passwd '*'
```

Adding Users to a Group

You can add users to the group by appending values to the *users* property with *nicl*'s *-merge* switch at the command line (or by using the *merge* command interactively). If the *users* property does not exist, *nicl* creates it. If the users are already part of the group, they are not added to the list (contrast this with the *-append* command, which can result in the same user being added more than once if the command is invoked multiple times).

```
# nicl / -merge /groups/writers users bjepson rothman
```

 To give someone administrative privileges, add that user to the *admin* group (*/groups/admin*). This gives him or her the ability to use *sudo* and install software that requires such privileges.

Listing Groups with nidump

Use *nidump* to confirm that the new group was created correctly. To list groups with *nidump*, pass in the format (in this case, the *group* file) and the domain (., the local domain).

```
% nidump group . | grep writers
writers:*:5005:bjepson,rothman
```

Because you can use *nireport* to dump any NetInfo directory, you could also use it to see this information:

```
% nireport . /groups name passwd gid users | grep writers
writers *        5005     bjepson,rothman
```

Deleting a Group

To delete a group, use *nicl*'s *-delete* switch. Be careful with this switch, since it will delete everything in and below the specified NetInfo directory:

```
# nicl / -delete /groups/writers
```

Managing Users and Passwords

The NetInfo equivalent of the *passwd* file resides under the */users* portion of the NetInfo directory. Mac OS X uses */etc/master.passwd* for storing encrypted passwords. That *master.passwd* file is called the *shadow password file* because it shadows the other, nonsensitive information contained in the */etc/passwd* file. Only the *root* user can read the shadow password file. Non-privileged users can use the regular *passwd* file to discover other information, such as a user's full name or home directory.

The *etc/passwd* and *etc/master.passwd* files are consulted only while the system is in single-user mode, or if the system has been reconfigured to use BSD Configuration Files (see the "Configuring Directory Services" section, earlier in this chapter). To add a normal user to your system, you should use System Preferences → Accounts. However, if you want to bulk-load NetInfo with many users or create a user while logged in over *ssh*, you can use *nicl* or *niload*.

You can list all users with the *nireport* utility. Supply the NetInfo domain (., the local domain), the directory (*/users*), and the properties you want to inspect (*uid, name, home, realname,* and *shell*):

```
% nireport . /users uid name home realname shell
-2      nobody  /dev/null           Unprivileged User       /dev/null
0       root    /var/root           System Administrator    /bin/tcsh
1       daemon  /var/root           System Services         /dev/null
99      unknown /dev/null           Unknown User            /dev/null
70      www     /Library/WebServer  World Wide Web Server    /dev/null
```

Creating a User with niload

The *niload* utility understands the flat file format used by */etc/passwd* (name: password:uid:gid:class:change:expire:gecos:home_dir:shell). See the *passwd(5)* manpage for a description of each field. To add a new user, create a file that adheres to that format and load it with *niload*. You can use a here document rather than a separate file. This example creates a user for Ernest Rothman with a UID of 701 and membership in the *staff* (GID 20) group:

```
# niload passwd . <<EOF
? rothman:*:701:20::0:0:Ernest Rothman:/Users/rothman:/bin/tcsh
? EOF
```

As you can see from this example, we set the password field to *, which disables logins for that account. To set the password, we'll use the *passwd* command to set it:

```
# passwd rothman
Changing password for rothman.
New password: ********
Retype new password: ********
```

If you *niload* a user that already exists, that user will not be overwritten or changed in any way. You should delete the user with *nicl* first (see the "Deleting a Group" section, earlier in this chapter). Before the user can log in, you must create his home directory (see the "Creating a User's Home Directory" section, later in this chapter).

Creating a User with nicl

To create a user with *nicl*, you'll need to create a directory under */users*, and set the *uid*, *gid*, *shell*, *realname*, and *home* properties. The following code creates the same user shown in the previous section, "Creating a User with niload."

```
# nicl / -create /users/rothman uid 701
# nicl / -create /users/rothman gid 20
# nicl / -create /users/rothman shell /bin/tcsh
# nicl / -create /users/rothman home /Users/rothman
# nicl / -create /users/rothman realname "Ernest Rothman"
# nicl / -create /users/rothman passwd \*
```

After you create the user, you should set the password as shown in the previous section.

Creating a User's Home Directory

One thing that NetInfo can't do for you is create the user's home directory. Mac OS X keeps a skeleton directory under the */System/Library/User Template* directory. If you look in this directory, you'll see localized versions of a user's home directory. To copy the localized English version of the home directory, use the *ditto* command:

```
# ditto /System/Library/User\ Template/English.lproj /Users/rothman
```

Then, use *chown* to recursively set the ownership of the home directory and all its contents (make sure you set the group to a group of which the user is a member):

```
# chown -R rothman:staff /Users/rothman
```

This change makes the new user the owner of his home directory and all its contents.

Modifying a User

You can change a user's properties by deleting a property with *-delete* and adding it again with *-create*. For example, to change *rothman*'s shell to *bash*, use:

```
# nicl / -delete /users/rothman shell
# nicl / -create /users/rothman shell /bin/bash
```

 You can also modify most user settings with System Preferences → Accounts.

Listing Users with nidump

Use *nidump* to confirm that *rothman* was added successfully. To list users with *nidump*, pass in the format (in this case, the *passwd* file) and the domain (use . for the local domain):

```
% nidump passwd . | grep rothman
rothman:nIhowm2pOBGsE:701:20::0:0:Ernest Rothman:/Users/rothman:/bin/tcsh
```

Deleting a User

To delete a user, use *nicl's* *-delete* switch. Since *-delete* recursively deletes everything under the specified directory, use this option with caution:

```
# nicl / -delete /users/rothman
```

If you want to also delete that user's home directory, you will have to do it manually, using *rm -r*.

Managing Hostnames and IP Addresses

Mac OS X 10.1 (and earlier versions of Mac OS X) only consulted */etc/hosts* in single-user mode and stored hostname/IP address mappings in the */machines* portion of the NetInfo database. As of Mac OS X 10.2, you can use the */etc/hosts* file to map hostnames to IP addresses. For example, the following entry would map the hostname *xyzzy* to 192.168.0.1:

```
192.168.0.1   xyzzy
```

Creating a Host with niload

If you are using Mac OS X 10.1.5 (or an earlier version of Mac OS X), you'll need to use NetInfo to maintain the hosts database. The *niload* utility understands the flat file format used by */etc/hosts* (ip_address:name). See the *hosts(5)* manpage for a description of each field. To add a new host, create a file using that format and load it with *niload*. This example uses a here document instead of a separate file to add the host *xyzzy*:

```
# niload hosts . <<EOF
? 192.168.0.1 xyzzy
? EOF
```

If you add an entry that already exists, it will not be changed or overwritten. Instead, *niload* will silently ignore your command. (To override this behavior, see the *-m* option under "niload" in the "NetInfo Command Reference" section, earlier in this chapter.)

Exporting Directories with NFS

Mac OS X 10.1 (and earlier versions of Mac OS X) stored NFS exports in the */exports* portion of the NetInfo directory. As of Mac OS X 10.2, however, you can use the */etc/exports* file. For example, the following line exports the */Users* directory to two hosts (192.168.0.134 and 192.168.0.106):

```
/Users  -ro -mapall=nobody 192.168.0.134 192.168.0.106
```

The NFS server will start automatically at boot time if there are any exports in the NetInfo database. After you've set up your exports, you can reboot, and NFS should start automatically. NFS options supported by Mac OS X include the following:

-maproot=user
> Specifies that the remote *root* user should be mapped to the specified user. You may specify either a username or numeric user ID.

-maproot=user:[group[:group...]]
> Specifies that the remote *root* user should be mapped to the specified user with the specified group credentials. If you include the colon with no groups, as in *-maproot=*username:, it means the remote user should have no group credentials. You may specify a username or numeric user ID for *user* and a group name or numeric group ID for *group*.

-mapall=user
> Specifies that all remote users should be mapped to the specified user.

-mapall=user:[group[:group...]]
> Specifies that all remote users should be mapped to the specified user with the specified group credentials. If you include the colon with no groups, as in *mapall=*username:, it specifies that the remote user should be given no group credentials.

-kerb
> Uses a Kerberos authentication server to authenticate and map client credentials.

-ro
> Exports the file system read-only. The synonym -o is also supported.

Flat Files and Their NetInfo Counterparts

As was mentioned earlier, NetInfo managed information for several flat files in earlier releases of Mac OS X, including */etc/printcap*, */etc/mail/aliases*, */etc/protocols*, and */etc/services*. For a complete list of known flat file formats, see the *nidump* and *niload* manpages.

Although you can edit these flat files directly as you would on any other Unix system, you can also use NetInfo to manage this information. You can use *niload* with a supported flat file format to add entries to NetInfo, or you can use *nicl* or NetInfo Manager to directly manipulate the entries. Table 3-2 lists each flat file, the corresponding portion of the NetInfo directory, and important properties associated with each entry. See the *netinfo(5)* manpage for complete details. Properties marked with (list) can take multiple values. (For an example, see the "Adding Users to a Group" section, earlier in this chapter).

The "Wired into Directory Services?" column in Table 3-2 indicates whether Directory Services will consult the flat file when the BSD configuration files plug-in is enabled. In some cases, an operating system daemon may bypass Directory Services and consult a flat file, and Directory Services then has no knowledge of the flat file. For example, *nfsd* can consult either Directory Services or */etc/exports*, but if it uses the flat file, it is consulting it directly and is not going through Directory Services.

Table 3-2. Flat files and their NetInfo counterparts

Flat file	NetInfo directory	Important properties	Wired into Directory Services?
/etc/exports	/exports	name, clients (list), opts (list)	No
/etc/fstab	/mounts	name, dir, type, opts (list), passno, freq	Yes
/etc/group	/groups	name, passwd, gid, users (list)	Yes
/etc/hosts	/machines	ip_address, name (list)	Yes
/etc/mail/aliases	/aliases	name, members (list)	No
/etc/networks	/networks	name (list), address	No
/etc/passwd, /etc/ master.passwd	/users	name, passwd, uid, gid, realname, home, shell	Yes
/etc/printcap	/printers	name, and various printcap properties (see the printcap(5) manpage)	No
/etc/protocols	/protocols	name (list), number	No
/etc/rpc	/rpcs	name (list), number	No
/etc/services	/services	name (list), port, protocol (list)	No

Restoring the NetInfo Database

If the NetInfo database is damaged, boot into single-user mode by holding down ⌘-S as the system starts up. Next, check to see if you have a backup of the NetInfo database. The */etc/daily cron* job backs up the NetInfo database each time it is run. You can find the backup in */var/backups/local.nidump*. If you don't have a backup, you won't be able to restore the NetInfo settings.

The *local.nidump* file is overwritten each time the *cron* job runs, so make sure you back it up regularly (preferably to some form of removable media).

 If your computer is generally not turned on at 3:15 a.m. (the default time for the *daily cron* job), you'll never get a backup of your NetInfo database. You can solve this problem by editing */etc/crontab* to run this job at a different time, or to run the job periodically with the command *sudo periodic daily*. See the "Default cron Jobs" section in Chapter 2 for more details.

After the system boots in single-user mode, you should:

1. Log in as the *root* user.
2. Fix any filesystem errors:

   `# /sbin/fsck -y`
3. Mount the *root* filesystem as read/write:

   `# /sbin/mount -uw /`
4. Change directories and go to the NetInfo database directory:

   `# cd /var/db/netinfo/`
5. Move the database out of the way and give it a different name:

   `# mv local.nidb/ local.nidb.broken`
6. Switch directories and go to the *StartupItems* directory:

   `# cd /System/Library/StartupItems`
7. Start the network:

   `# ./Network/Network start`
8. Start the port mapper, since NetInfo depends on it. Ignore any warnings about a missing NetInfo database:

   `# ./Portmap/Portmap start`
9. Start NetInfo. Since it has to rebuild the NetInfo database, this may take several minutes:

   `# ./DirectoryServices/DirectoryServices start`
10. Load the backup into NetInfo:

    `# /usr/bin/niload -d -r / . < /var/backups/local.nidump`
11. Create the *.AppleSetupDone* file so that the Setup Assistant does not appear when you reboot:

    `# touch /var/db/.AppleSetupDone`

After you have restored the NetInfo database, reboot the system with the *reboot* command.

## PART II

Building Applications

Although Apple's C compiler is based on the GNU Compiler Collection (GCC), there are important differences between compiling and linking on the Mac OS X and on other platforms. This part of the book describes these differences and explains how you can package applications for Mac OS X. Chapters in this part include:

- Chapter 4, *Compiling Source Code*
- Chapter 5, *Libraries, Headers, and Frameworks*
- Chapter 6, *Creating and Installing Packages*

Compiling Source Code

The Mac OS X Developer Tools are available from Apple and provide a development environment that will be familiar to any Unix developer who works with command-line compilers. For details about obtaining these tools, see the "Developer Tools" section in the Preface. The Developer Tools include all sorts of other goodies, including an advanced Integrated Development Environment (IDE), but coverage of those tools is beyond the scope and intent of this book. To learn more about the Developer Tools, you can see */Developer/Documentation/DeveloperTools/devtools.html*. You can also learn how to use Project Builder and Interface Builder and how to program Cocoa applications with Objective-C in *Learning Cocoa with Objective-C* (O'Reilly) and *Building Cocoa Applications: A Step-by-Step Guide* (O'Reilly).

The C compiler that comes with the Developer Tools is based on the Free Software Foundation's GNU Compiler Collection, or GCC. Apple's modifications to GCC include the addition of Objective-C to the compiler suite, as well as various modifications to deal with the Darwin operating system. The development environment in Mac OS X includes:

AppleScript
> This is an English-like language used to script applications and the operating system. AppleScript is installed as part of the Mac OS X operating system and does not require the Developer Tools package.

AppleScript Studio
> This is a high-level development environment based on AppleScript that allows you to build GUI applications by hooking AppleScript into the Cocoa frameworks. AppleScript Studio is installed along with the Developer Tools package.

Compilers
> These compilers are based on GCC and provide support for C, C++, Objective-C, Objective-C++, and assembly.

Compiler Tools

These include the Mac OS X Mach-O GNU-based assemblers, Mach-O static link editor, Mach-O dynamic link editor, and Mach-O object file tools, such as *nm* and *otool*.

Documentation

There is extensive documentation for the Apple Developer Tools (provided by Apple). Available in both HTML and PDF formats, the developer documentation can be found in */Developer/Documentation*. The documents are also available online from the Apple Developer Connection (ADC) web site (*http://connect.apple.com*).

 You can also access the documentation for GCC with your web browser by going to */Developer/Documentation/ DeveloperTools/Compiler/CompilerTOC.html*.

Debugger

The Apple debugger is based on GNU *gdb*.

Miscellaneous Tools

These include traditional development tools, such as GNU *make* and GNU *libtool*, graphical and command-line performance tools, Project Builder for WebObjects (Mac OS X Server), and an extensive set of Java development tools.

Project Builder

This is an integrated development environment for Mac OS X that supports Cocoa and Carbon programming with C, C++, Objective-C, and Java.

Interface Builder

This is a graphical user interface editor for Cocoa and Carbon applications.

We will not address the complete Mac OS X development suite in this chapter. Instead, we will focus on the command-line development tools and how they differ from the implementations on other Unix platforms.

Java programmers will find that the Mac OS X command-line Java tools (see "Java Development Tools" in Chapter 1) behave as they do under Unix and Linux.

Perl programmers coming from previous Macintosh systems will find that Mac OS X does not use MacPerl (*http://www.macperl.com*), but instead, uses the standard Unix build of the core Perl distribution (*http://www.perl.org*).

Compiler Differences

GCC is supported on a wide range of platforms and is familiar to most Unix developers. A natural consequence of this is that most Unix developers will find a familiar development environment in Mac OS X. There are, however, some important differences.

One difference that experienced GCC users may notice, particularly if they have dealt with a lot of mathematical and scientific programming, is that Mac OS X's Developer Tools do not include FORTRAN. However, the Fink distribution (*http://fink.sourceforge.net*) includes *g77*, the GNU FORTRAN '77 compiler. Also, the Darwin archive includes the source code for *g77*, which you can use to compile FORTRAN code. For more information on the Darwin CVS archive, see Chapter 7.

 Mac OS X's C compiler contains a number of Mac OS X-specific features that have not been folded into the main GCC distribution. (It is up to the Free Software Foundation (FSF) to accept and merge Apple's patches.) For information on how Apple's compiler differs from the GNU version, see the *README.Apple* file in the Darwin CVS archive's *gcc3* subdirectory.

As of this writing, Apple's *cc* compiler is based on GCC 3.1. However, GCC 2.95 is also available as */usr/bin/gcc2*. By default, invoking *cc* or *gcc* will invoke GCC 3.1. You can change this to GCC 2.95 by running the command *gcc_select 2*, and you can change it back with *gcc_select 3*. You can see the current settings by running *gcc_select* with no arguments:

```
% gcc_select
Apple Computer, Inc. GCC version 1161, based on gcc version 3.1
20020420 (prerelease)
```

 You can find the Mac OS X Compiler Release Notes on your system at */Developer/Documentation/ReleaseNotes/Compiler. html*. You should consult these release notes for details on the most current known problems, issues, and features.

AltiVec

The Motorola AltiVec Velocity Engine is also supported for G4 processors by the Mac OS X GCC implementation. The compiler flag *-faltivec* must be specified to compile code engineered to use the Velocity Engine. Inclusion of this command-line option to *cc* defines the preprocessor symbol _ _VEC_ _.

Compiling Unix Source Code

Many of the differences between Mac OS X and other versions of Unix become apparent when you try to build Unix-based software on Mac OS X. Most Unix-based open source software uses GNU *autoconf* or a similar facility, which generates a *configure* script that performs a number of tests of the system—especially of the installed Development Tools—and finishes by constructing one or more makefiles. After the *configure* script has done its job, you run the *make* command to first compile, and, if all goes well, install the resulting binaries.

> Most tarballs will include a *configure* script, so you do not need to generate it yourself. However, if you retrieve *autoconf*-managed source code from a CVS archive, you will have to run *autoconf.sh* manually to generate the *configure* file.

In most cases, performing the following three steps is all that is needed to successfully compile a Unix-based application on Mac OS X after you have unpacked the tarball and changed to the top-level source code directory:

```
./configure
make
make install
```

> Mac OS X web browsers are configured to invoke StuffIt on compressed archives. So, if you click on a link to a tarball, you may find that it gets downloaded to your desktop and extracted there. If you'd prefer to manage the download and extraction process yourself, Control-click or right-click on the link so you can specify a download location.

The following sections deal with issues involved in successfully performing these steps. Determining how to improvise within that three-step procedure reveals some of the differences between Mac OS X and other Unix systems.

The First Line of Defense

Most tarballs will include the following files in the top-level directory: *README*, *INSTALL*, and a file named *PORT* or *PORTING*. These files contain useful information that may help you get the application running on Mac OS X.

README

This document is an introduction to the application and source code. Also, you'll often find copyright information in this document, notes about bug fixes or improvements made to different versions of the application, and pointers to web sites, FAQs, and mailing lists.

INSTALL

This document contains step-by-step installation instructions.

PORT or *PORTING*

If present, one of these documents will include tips for porting the application to another platform.

Host Type

One of the first difficulties you may encounter in running a *configure* script is when the script aborts with an error message stating that the host system cannot be determined.

Strictly speaking, the *host type* refers to the system on which software will run, and the *build type* refers to the system on which the software is being built. It is possible to build software on one system to run on another system, but to do so requires a cross-compiler. We will not concern ourselves with cross-compiler issues. Thus, for our discussion, both the host type and the build (and target) types are the same: `powerpc-apple-darwinVERSION`, where the `VERSION` denotes the particular version of Darwin. In fact, a *configure* script detects Mac OS X by the host/build type named *Darwin,* since Darwin is the actual operating system underlying Mac OS X. This can be verified by issuing the *uname -v* command, which tells you that you're running a Darwin kernel, the kernel version, and when it was last built.

Many *configure* scripts are designed to determine the host system, since the resulting makefiles will differ depending on the type of system for which the software is being built. The *configure* script is designed to be used with two files related to the host type, usually residing in the same directory as the *configure* script. These files are *config.guess*, which is used to help guess the host type; and *config.sub*, which is used to validate the host type and to put it into a canonical form (such as *CPUTYPE-MANUFACTURER-OS*, as in `powerpc-apple-darwin6.0`).

Since Mac OS X and Darwin are relatively new, you may run across source code distributions that contain older *config.** files that don't work with Mac OS X. You can find out if these files support Darwin by running the *./configure* script. If the script complains about an unknown host type, you know that you have a set of *config.** files that don't support Darwin.

In that case, you can replace the *config.guess* and *config.sub* files with the Apple-supplied, like-named versions residing in */usr/share/automake-1.6*. These replacement files originate from the FSF and include the code necessary to configure a source tree for Mac OS X. To copy these files into the *source* directory, which contains the *configure* script, simply issue the following commands from within the *sources* directory:

```
cp /usr/share/automake-1.6/config.sub .
cp /usr/share/automake-1.6/config.guess .
```

Macros

You can use a number of predefined macros to detect Apple systems and Mac OS X in particular. For example, `__APPLE__` is a macro that is defined on every Apple *gcc*-based Mac OS X system, and `__MACH__` is one of several macros specific to Mac OS X. Table 4-1 lists the predefined macros available on Mac OS X.

Table 4-1. Mac OS X C macros

Macro	When defined
`__OBJC__`	When the compiler is compiling Objective-C *.m* files or Objective-C++ *.M* files. (To override the file extension, use *-ObjC* or *-ObjC++*).
`__ASSEMBLER__`	When the compiler is compiling *.s* files.
`__NATURAL_ALIGNMENT__`	When compiling for systems that use natural alignment, such as *powerpc*.
`__STRICT_BSD__`	If, and only if, the *-bsd* flag is specified as an argument to the compiler.
`__MACH__`	When compiling for systems that support Mach system calls.
`__APPLE__`	When compiling for any Apple system. Currently defined only on Mac OS X systems running Apple's variant of the GNU C compiler. Do not rely on this macro to tell you that you are on Darwin or Mac OS X, since third-party compilers may not define this macro.
`__APPLE_CC__`	When compiling for any Apple system. Integer value that corresponds to the (Apple) version of the compiler.
`__VEC__`	When AltiVec support was enabled with the *-faltivec* flag.

Do not rely on the presence of the `__APPLE__` macro to determine which compiler features or libraries are supported. Instead, we suggest that you use a package like GNU *autoconf* to tell you which features the target operating system supports. This approach makes it more likely that your applications can compile out-of-the-box (or with little effort) on operating systems to which you don't have access.

Supported Languages

When using the *cc* command, which supports more than one language, the language is determined by either the filename suffix or by explicitly specifying the language using the *-x* option. Table 4-2 lists some of the more commonly used filename suffixes and *-x* arguments supported by Apple's version of GCC.

Table 4-2. File suffixes recognized by cc

File suffix	Language	-x argument
.c	C source code to be preprocessed and compiled	c
.C, .cc, .cxx, .cpp	C++ source code to be preprocessed and compiled	c++
.h	C header that should neither be compiled nor linked	c-header
.i	C source code that should be compiled but not preprocessed	cpp-output
.ii	Objective-C++ or C++ source code that should be compiled but not preprocessed	c++-cpp-output
.m	Objective-C source code	objective-c
.M, .mm	Mixed Objective-C++ and Objective-C source code	objective-c++
.s	Assembler source that should be assembled but not preprocessed	assembler
.S	Assembler source to be preprocessed and assembled	assembler-with-cpp

Although the HFS+ filesystem is case-insensitive, the *cc* compile driver recognizes the uppercase C in a source file. For example, *cc foo.C* invokes *cc*'s C++ compiler because the file extension is an uppercase C, which denotes a C++ source file. (To *cc*, it's just a command-line argument.) So, even though HFS+ will find the same file whether you type *cc foo.c* or *cc foo.C*, what you enter on the command line makes all the difference in the world, particularly to *cc*.

Preprocessing

When you invoke *cc* without options, it initiates a sequence of four basic operations, or stages: preprocessing, compilation, assembly, and linking. In a multifile program, the first three stages are performed on each individual source code file, creating an object code file for each source code file. The final linking stage combines all the object codes that were created by the first three stages, along with user-specified object code that may have been compiled earlier into a single executable image file.

Apple's compiler provides two preprocessors. The default preprocessor for both C and Objective-C is the *precompilation preprocessor* written by Apple, named *cpp-precomp*. The standard GNU C preprocessor, named *cpp*, is also available and is the default for Objective-C++ code. *cpp-precomp* supports precompiled header files. (For more information about *cpp-precomp*, see Chapter 5.) *cpp-precomp* is faster than *cpp*. However, some code may not compile with *cpp-precomp*. In that case, you should invoke *cpp* by instructing *cc* not to use *cpp-precomp*. For example, to compile the C program *myprog.c* using the standard GNU preprocessor, *cpp*, use the *-no-cpp-precomp* switch as follows:

```
cc -no-cpp-precomp myprog.c
```

 Earlier versions of the Mac OS X Developer Tools used the *-traditional-cpp* switch, but this switch had undesirable side effects and is deprecated.

Chapter 5 describes precompilation in more detail.

Frameworks

Object-oriented frameworks are critical in Mac OS X. Indeed Cocoa, the object-oriented toolkit for user interface development, consists of the Foundation and Application Kit (or AppKit) frameworks for Objective-C and Java. It is often necessary to let the preprocessor know where to search for framework header files. You can do this with the *-F* option, which is also accepted by the linker. Thus:

```
-F directoryname
```

instructs the preprocessor to search the directory *directoryname* for framework header files. The search begins in *directoryname* and, if necessary, continues in order in the following standard framework directories:

- */Library/Frameworks* (if the *-no-cpp-precomp* flag is specified)
- */System/Library/Frameworks*

To include a framework object header in Objective-C, use #import. The format of the #import preprocessor directive in your Objective-C code is:

```
#import <frameworkname/headerfilename.h>
```

Here, *frameworkname* is the name of the framework without the extension, and *headerfilename*.h is the source for the header file.

The *-F* option is accepted by the preprocessor and the linker, and is used in either case to specify directories in which to search for framework header files. (This is similar to the *-I* option, which specifies directories to search for *.h* files.) By default, the linker searches the standard directories, */Local/ Library/Frameworks* and */System/Library/Frameworks*, for frameworks. The directory search order can be modified with *-F* options. For example:

```
cc -F dir1 -F dir2 -no-cpp-precomp myprog.c
```

will result in *dir1* being searched first, followed by *dir2*, followed by the standard framework directories. The other flag pertaining to frameworks is *-framework*. Inclusion of this flag results in a search for the specified framework named when linking. Example 4-1 shows "Hello, World" in Objective-C. Notice that it #imports the AppKit framework.

Example 4-1. Saying hello from Objective-C

```
#import <Appkit/AppKit.h>

int main(int argc, const char *argv[])
{
  NSLog(@"Hello, World\n");
  return 0;
}
```

Save Example 4-1 as *hello.m*. To compile it, use *-framework* to pass in the framework name:

```
cc -framework AppKit -o hello hello.m
```

The *-framework* flag is accepted only by the linker and is used to name a framework. The flag *-nostdinc* is used to prohibit the search for header files in any directory other than those specified via other options, such as *-I*. Since strict ANSI-C does not allow many of the preprocessor constructs used in most software created nowadays, the preprocessors are designed to allow several nonstandard ANSI-C constructs by default. Although it is usually undesirable to do so, you must include the compile driver flags *-trigraphs*, *-undef*, and *-pedantic* to enforce strict ANSI-C standards .

There are also several undocumented features of the compiler. These include the following *cc* command-line flags.

-fpascal-strings
> A flag that enables the compiler to recognize Pascal strings

-Wmost
> A Darwin-specific compiler flag, equivalent to *-Wall,* with the exception that it does not turn on *-Wparenthesis*

Other compiler flags of particular interest in Mac OS X are related to the peculiarities of building shared code. For more details, see Chapter 5.

Architectural Issues

There are a few architectural issues to be aware of when developing or porting software on Mac OS X. In particular, pointer size, endian-ness, and inline assembly code tend to be the most common issues.

On a 32-bit system, such as Mac OS X running on the G3 or G4, C pointers are 32 bits (4 bytes). On a 64-bit system, they are 64 bits (8 bytes). As long as your code does not rely on any assumptions about pointer size, it should be 64-bit clean. For example, on a 32-bit system, the following program prints "4", and on a 64-bit system, it prints "8":

```
#include <stdio.h>
int main( )
{
  printf("%d\n", sizeof(void *));
}
```

Some 64-bit operating systems, such as Solaris 8 on Ultra hardware (sun4u), have a 64-bit kernel space, but support both 32- and 64-bit mode applications, depending on how they are compiled.

CPU architectures are designed to treat the bytes of words in memory as being arranged in big or little endian order. Big endian ordering has the most significant byte in the lowest address, while little endian has the most significant byte at the highest byte address.

The PowerPC is bi-endian, meaning that the CPU is instructed at boot time to order memory as either big or little endian. Additionally, the PowerPC architecture can also switch endian-ness at runtime, although this is generally not done. In practice, bi-endian CPUs run exclusively as big or little endian. In general, Intel architectures are little-endian, while most, but not all, Unix/RISC machines are big-endian. Table 4-3 summarizes the endian-ness of various CPU architectures and operating systems.

Table 4-3. Endian-ness of some operating systems

CPU type	Operating system	Endian-ness
Dec Alpha	Digital Unix	little-endian
Dec Alpha	VMS	little-endian
Hewlett Packard PA-RISC	HP-UX	big-endian
IBM RS/6000	AIX	big-endian
Intel x86	Windows	little-endian
Intel x86	Linux	little-endian
Intel x86	Solaris x86	little-endian
Motorola PowerPC	Mac OS X	big-endian

Table 4-3. Endian-ness of some operating systems (continued)

CPU type	Operating system	Endian-ness
Motorola PowerPC	Linux	big-endian
SGI R4000 and up	IRIX	big-endian
Sun SPARC	Solaris	big-endian

As far as inline assembly code is concerned—if you've got any—it will have to be lovingly rewritten by hand. Heaven help you if you have to port a whole Just-In-Time (JIT) compiler! For information on the assembler and PowerPC machine language, see the Mac OS X Assembler Guide (*/Developer/ Documentation/DeveloperTools/Assembler/AssemblerTOC.html*).

Libraries, Headers, and Frameworks

In this chapter, we discuss the linking phase of building Unix-based software under Mac OS X. In particular, we discuss header files in Mac OS X and libraries.

Header Files

There are two types of header files in Mac OS X.

Ordinary header files
    These header files are inserted into source code by a preprocessor prior to compilation. Ordinary header files have a *.h* extension.

Precompiled header files
    These header files have a *.p* extension.

Header files serve four functions:

- They contain C declarations.
- They contain macro definitions.
- They provide for conditional compilation.
- They provide line control when combining multiple source files into a single file that is subsequently compiled.

 The mechanism for enabling strict *POSIX.1* compliance is built into the system header files. The preprocessor variables _ANSI_SOURCE, __STRICT_ANSI__, and _POSIX_SOURCE are supported.

Unix developers will find the ordinary header files familiar, since they follow the BSD convention. The C preprocessor directive #include includes a header file in a C source file. There are essentially three forms of this syntax:

```
#include <headername.h>
```
This form is used when the header file is located in the directory */usr/ include*.
```
#include <directory/headername.h>
```
This form is used when the header file is located in the directory */usr/ include/directory*, where *directory* is a subdirectory of */usr/include*.
```
#include "headername.h"
```
This form is used when the header file is located in a user or nonstandard directory. The form should either be in the same directory as the source file you are compiling or in a directory specified by *cc*'s *-Idirectory* switch.

You can use #include, followed by a macro, which, when expanded, must be in one of the aforementioned forms.

As noted in the previous chapter, frameworks in Mac OS X are common when you step outside of the BSD portions of the operating system. You must use #import instead of #include when working with a framework. To include a framework header file in Objective-C code, use the following format:

```
#import <frameworkname/headerfilename.h>
```

where *frameworkname* is the name of the framework without the extension and *headerfilename* is the name of the header file. For example, the included declaration for a Cocoa application would look like:

```
#import <Cocoa/Cocoa.h>
```

When preprocessing header files or any preprocessor directives, the following three actions are always taken:

- Comments are replaced by a single space.
- Any backslash line continuation escape symbol is removed and the line following it is joined with the current line. For example:

```
#def\
ine \
NMAX 2000
```

is processed as:

```
#define NMAX 2000
```

- Any predefined macro name is replaced with its expression. In Mac OS X, there are both standard ANSI C predefined macros, as well as several predefined macros specific to Mac OS X. For example, __APPLE_CC__ is replaced by an integer that represents the compiler's version number.

The following rules must be kept in mind:

- The preprocessor does not recognize comments or macros placed between the < and > in an #include directive.

- Comments placed within string constants are regarded as part of the string constant and are not recognized as C comments.

- If ANSI trigraph preprocessing is enabled with *cc -trigraph*, you must not use a backslash continuation escape symbol within a trigraph sequence, or the trigraph will not be interpreted correctly. ANSI trigraphs are three-character sequences that represent characters that may not be available on older terminals. For example, ??< translates to {. ANSI trigraphs are a rare occurrence these days.

Precompiled Header Files

Mac OS X's Developer Tools support and provide extensive documentation on building and using precompiled header files. This section highlights a few of the issues that may be of interest to Unix developers new to Mac OS X when it comes to working with precompiled headers.

Precompiled header files are binary files that have been generated from ordinary C header files and that have been preprocessed and parsed using *cpp-precomp*. When such a precompiled header is created, both macros and declarations present in the corresponding ordinary header file are sorted, resulting in a faster compile time, a reduced symbol table size, and consequently, faster lookup. Precompiled header files are given a *.p* extension and are produced from ordinary header files that end with a *.h* extension. There is no risk that a precompiled header file will get out of sync with the *.h* file, because the compiler checks the timestamp of the actual header file.

When using precompiled header files, you should not refer to the *.p* version of the name, but rather to the *.h* version in the #include directive. If a precompiled version of the header file is available, it will be used automatically; otherwise, the real header file (*.h*) will be used. So, to include *foo.p*, you would specify *foo.h*. The fact that *cc* is using a precompiled header is totally hidden from you.

In addition to checking the timestamp, the preprocessor also checks whether or not the current context is the same as the context in which the precompilation was performed. For the precompiled header to be used, the timestamp would need to indicate that the modification time of the *.p* version is more recent than the *.h* version, and therefore, that the contexts must be equivalent. The context is the amalgamation of all defines (#define) in place at the time you compile a program. If the defines are different the next time you include the *.h* file, *cpp-precomp* will regenerate the *.p* file based on the current set of defines.

Mac OS X system headers are precompiled. For example, *AppKit.p*, *Cocoa.p*, *mach.p*, and other precompiled header files are stored in */System/Library/ Frameworks*. You can create your own precompiled header files using the *cc -precomp* compile driver flag. For example, the following command illustrates this process in its simplest, context-independent form:

```
cc -precomp header.h -o header.p
```

If there is context dependence—for example, some conditional compilation—the *-Dsymbol* flag is used. In this case, the command to build a precompiled header file (with the *FOO* symbol defined) would be:

```
cc -precomp -DFOO header.h -o header.p
```

For more details on building and using precompiled header files, as well as using the *cpp-precomp* preprocessor, read the documentation stored in */Developer/Documentation/DeveloperTools/Preprocessor/*.

Although the *cpp-precomp* and the standard GNU *cpp* preprocessors are similar in function, there are several incompatibilities. For this reason, you will find it is often necessary to use the *-no-cpp-precomp* switch when porting Unix-based software to Mac OS X.

A complete list of precompiled headers can be found in the *phase1. precompList* and *phase2.precompList* files, located in */System/Library/System-Resources/PrecompLists*. Table 5-1 lists the contents of the files.

Table 5-1. Precompiled header files as listed in phase1.precompList and phase2. precompList

Precompiled headers	Filesystem location
phase1.precompList	
libc.p	/usr/include
unistd.p	/usr/include
mach.p	/usr/include/mach
phase2.precompList	
CoreServices.p	/System/Library/Frameworks/CoreServices.framework/Versions/A/Headers
CoreServices.pp	/System/Library/Frameworks/CoreServices.framework/Versions/A/Headers
ApplicationServices.p	/System/Library/Frameworks/ApplicationServices.framework/Versions/A/Headers
ApplicationServices.pp	/System/Library/Frameworks/ApplicationServices.framework/Versions/A/Headers

Table 5-1. Precompiled header files as listed in phase1.precompList and phase2. precompList (continued)

Precompiled headers	Filesystem location
phase2.precompList	
Carbon.p	/System/Library/Frameworks/Carbon.framework/Versions/A/Headers
Carbon.pp	/System/Library/Frameworks/Carbon.framework/Versions/A/Headers
Foundation.p	/System/Library/Frameworks/Foundation.framework/Versions/C/Headers
Foundation.pp	/System/Library/Frameworks/Foundation.framework/Versions/C/Headers
AppKit.p	/System/Library/Frameworks/AppKit.framework/Versions/C/Headers
AppKit.pp	/System/Library/Frameworks/AppKit.framework/Versions/C/Headers
Cocoa.p	/System/Library/Frameworks/Cocoa.framework/Versions/A/Headers
Cocoa.pp	/System/Library/Frameworks/Cocoa.framework/Versions/A/Headers

Although the filenames in *phase1.precompList* and *phase2.precompList* are listed as *filename.p* (for example, *libc.p*), the actual file used depends on the compiler version. For example, *gcc3* will use *libc-gcc3.p*. (Mac OS X 10.2 does not ship with precompiled heaeder files for *gcc2*.)

> The *.pp* files referred to in *phase2.precompList* are not present on the system, but the *gcc3* versions can be generated by running *sudo fixPrecomps -gcc3all*.

PFE precompilation

The *gcc3* compiler supports an alternative precompilation mechanism called Persistent Front End (PFE). This mechanism offers the same performance benefits as *cpp-precomp*, but supports C++ and Objective-C++. (*cpp-precomp* does not support either language.) To precompile a header file with PFE, compile the header, specifying the *--dump-pch* switch with the name of the output file. You'll also need to supply the language with the *-x* switch (see "Supported Languages" in Chapter 4):

```
gcc -x c --dump-pch header.pfe header.h
```

Then, you can compile *main.c* using the *--load-pch* switch, supplying the name of the precompiled file:

```
gcc --load-pch header.pfe main.c -o main
```

Example 5-1 shows *header.h*, and Example 5-2 shows *main.c*.

Example 5-1. The header.h file

```
/* header.h: a trivial header file. */

#define x 100
```

Example 5-2. The main.c application

```
/* main.c: a simple program that includes header.h. */

#include <stdio.h>
#include "header.h"

int main( )
{
  printf("%d\n", x);
  return 0;
}
```

malloc.h

make may fail in compiling some types of Unix software if it cannot find *malloc.h*. Software designed for older Unix systems may expect to find this header file in */usr/include*; however, *malloc.h* is not present in this directory. The set of malloc( ) function prototypes is actually found in *stdlib.h*. For portability, your programs should include *stdlib.h* instead of *malloc.h*. (This is the norm; systems that require you to use *malloc.h* are the rare exception these days.) GNU *autoconf* will detect systems that require *malloc.h* and define the HAVE_MALLOC_H macro. If you do not use GNU *autoconf*, you will need to detect this case on your own and set the macro accordingly. You can handle such cases with this code:

```
#include <stdlib.h>
#ifdef HAVE_MALLOC_H
#include <malloc.h>
#endif
```

For a list of libraries that come with Mac OS X, see the "Interesting and Important Libraries" section, later in this chapter.

The System Library: libSystem

In Darwin, much is built into the system library, */usr/lib/libSystem.dylib*. In particular, the following libraries are included in *libSystem*.

libc
> The standard C library. This library contains the functions used by C programmers on all platforms.

libinfo
> The NetInfo library.

libkvm
> The kernel virtual memory library.

libm

> The math library, which contains arithmetic functions.

libpthread

> The POSIX threads library, which allows multiple tasks to run concurrently within a single program.

Symbolic links are provided as placeholders for these libraries. For example, *libm.dylib* is a symbolic link in */usr/lib* that points to *libSystem.dylib*. Thus, *-lm* or *-lpthread* do no harm, but are unnecessary. The *-lm* option links to the math library, and *-lpthread* links to the POSIX threads library. Since *libSystem* provides these functions, you don't need to use these options. However, you should use them to make sure your application is portable to other systems. (Since *libm.dylib* and *libpthread.dylib* are symbolic links to *libSystem.dylib*, the extra *-l* options will refer to the same library.)

> In Mac OS X 10.1 and earlier versions, the *curses* screen library (a set of functions for controlling a terminal display) was part of *libSystem.dylib*. In Mac OS X 10.2 (Jaguar), the *ncurses* library (*/usr/lib/libncurses.5.dylib*) took the place of *curses*. You may still encounter source code releases that look for curses in *libSystem.dylib*, which will result in linking errors. You can work around this problem by adding *-lcurses* to the linker arguments. This is portable to earlier versions of Mac OS X as well, since */usr/lib/libcurses.dylib* is a symlink to *libncurses* in 10.2, and to *libSystem* in earlier versions.

Interestingly enough, there is no symbolic link for *libutil*, whose functionality is also provided by *libSystem*. (*libutil* is a library that provides functions related to login, logout, terminal assignment, and logging.) So, if a link fails because of *-lutil*, you should try taking it out to see if it solves the problem.

Shared Libraries Versus Loadable Modules

The Executable and Linking Format (ELF), developed by the Unix System Laboratories, is common in the Unix world. On ELF systems, there is no distinction between shared libraries and loadable modules; shared code can be used as a library for dynamic loading. ELF is the default binary format on Linux, Solaris 2.*x*, and SVR4. Since these systems cover a large share of the Unix base, most Unix developers have experience on ELF systems. Thus, it may come as a surprise to experienced Unix developers that shared libraries and loadable modules are not the same on Mac OS X. This is because the binary format used in Mac OS X is *Mach-O*, which is different from ELF.

Mach-O shared libraries have the file type MH_DYLIB and the *.dylib* (dynamic library) suffix and can be linked to with static linker flags. So, if you have a shared library named *libcool.dylib*, you can link to this library by specifying the *-lcool* flag. Although shared libraries cannot be loaded dynamically as modules, they can be loaded through the *dyld* API (see the manpage for *dyld*, the dynamic link editor). It is important to point out that shared libraries cannot be unloaded.

Loadable modules, called *bundles* in Mac OS X, have the file type MH_BUNDLE. Most Unix-based software ports usually produce bundles with a *.so* extension, for the sake of consistency across platforms. Although Apple recommends giving bundles a *.bundle* extension, it isn't mandatory.

 You cannot link directly against a bundle. Instead, bundles must be dynamically loaded and unloaded by the *dyld* APIs. When porting Unix-based software, you'll often need to translate dlopen( ) function calls to *dylib* actions. You can implement a temporary fix by using the *dlcompat* library from the Fink distribution, but the ideal solution is to do a complete port using the *dyld* APIs.

You need to use special flags with *cc* when compiling a shared library or a bundle on Darwin. One difference between Darwin and many other Unix systems is that no *position-independent code* (PIC) flag is needed, since it is the default for Darwin. Next, since the linker does not allow common symbols, the compiler flag *-fno-common* is required for both shared libraries and bundles. (A common symbol is one that is defined multiple times. You should instead define a symbol once and use C's *extern* keyword to declare it in places where it is needed.)

To build a shared library, use *cc*'s *-dynamiclib* option. Use the *-bundle* option to build a loadable module or bundle.

Building a Shared Library

Suppose you want to create a shared library containing one or more C functions, such as the one shown in Example 5-3.

Example 5-3. A simple C program

```
/*
 * answer.c: The answer to life, the universe, and everything.
 */
int get_answer( )
{
  return 42;
}
```

If you compile the program containing the function into a shared library, you could test it with the program shown in Example 5-4.

Example 5-4. Compiling answer.c into a shared library

```
/*
 * deep_thought.c: Obtain the answer to life, the universe,
 * and everything, and act startled when you actually hear it.
 */
#include <stdio.h>
int main( )
{
  int the_answer;
  the_answer = get_answer( );
  printf("The answer is... %d\n", the_answer);

  fprintf(stderr, "%d??!!\n", the_answer);
  return 0;
}
```

The *makefile* shown in Example 5-5 will compile and link the library, and then compile, link, and execute the test program.

Example 5-5. Sample makefile for creating and testing a shared library

```
# Makefile: Create and test a shared library.
#
# Usage: make test
#
CC = cc
LD = cc
CFLAGS = -O -fno-common

all: deep_thought

# Create the shared library.
#
answer.o: answer.c          .
        $(CC) $(CFLAGS) -c answer.c

libanswer.dylib: answer.o
        $(LD) -dynamiclib -install_name libanswer.dylib \
        -o libanswer.dylib answer.o

# Test the shared library with the deep_thought program.
#
deep_thought.o: deep_thought.c
        $(CC) $(CFLAGS) -c deep_thought.c

deep_thought: deep_thought.o libanswer.dylib
        $(LD) -o deep_thought deep_thought.o -L. -lanswer
```

Example 5-5. Sample makefile for creating and testing a shared library (continued)

```
test: all
        ./deep_thought

clean:
        rm -f *.o core deep_thought libanswer.dylib
```

Dynamically Loading Libraries

You can turn *answer.o* into a bundle, which can be dynamically loaded using the commands shown in Example 5-6.

Example 5-6. Commands for converting answer.o into a bundle

```
cc -flat_namespace -bundle -undefined suppress \
  -o libanswer.bundle answer.o
```

You do not need to specify the bundle at link time. Instead, use the *dyld* functions NSCreateObjectFileImageFromFile and NSLinkModule to load the library. Then, you can use NSLookupSymbolInModule and NSAddressOfSymbol to access the symbols that the library exports. Example 5-7 loads *libanswer. bundle* and invokes the get_answer function. Example 5-7 is similar to Example 5-4, but many lines (shown in **bold**) have been added.

Example 5-7. Dynamically loading a bundle and invoking a function

```
/*
 * deep_thought_dyld.c: Obtain the answer to life, the universe,
 * and everything, and act startled when you actually hear it.
 */
#include <stdio.h>
#import <mach-o/dyld.h>

int main( )
{
  int the_answer;
  int rc;                  // Success or failure result value
  NSObjectFileImage img;   // Represents the bundle's object file
  NSModule handle;         // Handle to the loaded bundle
  NSSymbol sym;            // Represents a symbol in the bundle

  int (*get_answer) (void);  // Function pointer for get_answer

  /* Get an object file for the bundle. */
  rc = NSCreateObjectFileImageFromFile("libanswer.bundle", &img);
  if (rc != NSObjectFileImageSuccess) {
    fprintf(stderr, "Could not load libanswer.bundle.\n");
    exit(-1);
  }
```

```
/* Get a handle for the bundle. */
handle = NSLinkModule(img, "libanswer.bundle", FALSE);

/* Look up the get_answer function. */
sym = NSLookupSymbolInModule(handle, "_get_answer");
if (sym == NULL)
{
   fprintf(stderr, "Could not find symbol: _get_answer.\n");
   exit(-2);
}

/* Get the address of the function. */
get_answer = NSAddressOfSymbol(sym);

/* Invoke the function and display the answer. */
the_answer = get_answer( );
printf("The answer is... %d\n", the_answer);

fprintf(stderr, "%d??!!\n", the_answer);
return 0;
}
```

For more information on these functions, see the `NSObjectFileImage`, `NSModule`, and `NSSymbol` manpages. To compile the code in Example 5-7, use the following command:

```
cc  -O -fno-common -o deep_thought_dyld deep_thought_dyld.c
```

Two-level Namespaces

In Mac OS X 10.0, the dynamic linker merged symbols into a single (flat) namespace. So, if you link against two different libraries that both define the same function, the dynamic linker complains, because the same symbol was defined in both places. This approach prevented collisions that were known at compile time. However, if there wasn't a conflict at compile time, there is no guarantee that a future version of the library won't introduce a conflict.

Suppose you linked your application against version 1 of *libfoo* and version 1 of *libbar*. At the time you compiled your application, *libfoo* defined a function called `logerror( )`, and *libbar* did not. But when version 2 of *libbar* came out, it included a function called `logerror( )`. Since the conflict was not known at compile time, your application doesn't expect *libbar* to contain this function. If your application happens to load *libbar* before *libfoo*, it will call *libbar*'s `logerror( )` method, which is not what you want.

So, Mac OS X 10.1 introduced two-level namespaces, which the compiler uses by default. (Mac OS X 10.2 does not introduce any changes to two-level namespaces.) With this feature, you can link against version 1 of *libfoo* and

---

libbar. The linker creates an application that knows logerror( ) lives in *lib-foo*. So, even if a future version of *libbar* includes a logerror( ) function, your application will know which logerror( ) it should use.

If you want to build an application using a flat namespace, use the *-flat_namespace* linker flag. See the *ld* manpage for more details.

Library Versions

Library version numbering is one area where Mac OS X differs from other Unix variants. In particular, the dynamic linker *dyld* checks both major and minor version numbers. Also, the manner in which library names carry the version numbers is different. On ELF systems, shared libraries are named with an extension similar to the following:

```
libname.so.major_version_no.minor_version_no
```

Typically, a symbolic link is created in the library named *libname.so*, which points to the most current version of the library. For example, on an ELF system like Solaris, *libMagick.so.5.0.44* is the name of an actual library. If this is the latest installed version of the library, you can find symbolic links that point to this library in the same directory. These symbolic links are typically created during the installation process.

In this example, both *libMagick.so* and *libMagick.so.5* are symbolic links that point to *libMagick.so.5.0.44*. Older versions of the library may also be present, such as *libMagick.so.5.0.42*. However, although older versions of the library may be present, whenever a newer version is installed, the symbolic links are updated to point to the latest version. This works because when you create a shared library, you need to specify the name of the library to be used when the library is called by a program at runtime.

 In general, you should keep older versions of libraries around, just in case an application depends on them. If you are certain there are no dependencies, you can safely remove an older version.

On Mac OS X, the *libMagick* library is named *libMagick.5.0.44.dylib*, and the symbolic links *libMagick.dylib* and *libMagick.5.dylib* point to it. Older versions, such as *libMagick.5.0.42.dylib*, may also be found in the same directory. One difference that is immediately apparent on Mac OS X systems is that the version numbers are placed between the library name and the *.dylib* extension rather than at the end of the filename, as on other Unix systems (e.g., *libMagick.so.5.0.42*).

Another difference on Darwin is that the absolute pathname is specified when the library is installed. Thus, *ldconfig* is not used in Darwin, since paths to linked dynamic shared libraries are included in the executables. On an ELF system, you typically use *ldconfig* or set the LD_LIBRARY_PATH variable. In Darwin, use DYLD_LIBRARY_PATH instead of LD_LIBRARY_PATH (see the *dyld* man page for more details).

You can link against a particular version of a library by including the appropriate option for *cc*, such as *-lMagick.5.0.42*. Minor version checking is another way that the Mach-O format differs from ELF. To illustrate this, let's revisit Example 5-4, earlier in this chapter.

Suppose that the library shown in Example 5-4 will continue to be improved over time; minor bugs will be fixed, minor expanded capabilities will be added, and, in time, major new features will be added. In each of these cases, there will be a need to rename the library to reflect the latest version. Assume that the last version of the library is named *libanswer.1.2.5.dylib*. The major version number is *1*, the minor revision is *2*, and the bug-fix (i.e., fully compatible) revision number is *5*. Example 5-8 illustrates how to update this library to release *libanswer.1.2.6.dylib,* which is fully compatible with the release 1.2.5, but contains some bug fixes.

In the *makefile* shown earlier in Example 5-5, replace the following lines:

```
libanswer.dylib: answer.o
        $(LD) -dynamiclib -install_name libanswer.dylib \
        -o libanswer.dylib answer.o
```

with the code shown in Example 5-8.

Example 5-8. Versioning the answer library

```
libanswer.dylib: answer.o
    $(LD) -dynamiclib -install_name libanswer.1.dylib \
        -compatibility_version 1.2 -current_version 1.2.6 \
            -o libanswer.1.2.6.dylib  $(OBJS)
    rm -f libanswer.1.dylib    libanswer.1.2.dylib  libanswer.dylib
    ln -s libanswer.1.2.6.dylib libanswer.1.2.dylib
    ln -s libanswer.1.2.6.dylib libanswer.1.dylib
    ln -s libanswer.1.2.6.dylib libanswer.dylib
```

Symbolic links are established to point to the actual library: one link reflecting the major revision, one reflecting the minor revision, and one that simply reflects the name of the library.

The compatibility version number checks that the library used by an executable is compatible with the library that was linked in creating the executable. This is why the phrase *compatibility version* makes sense in this context.

Creating and Linking Static Libraries

The creation of static libraries in Mac OS X is much the same as in Unix variants, with one exception. After installation in the destination directory, *ranlib* must be used to recatalog the newly installed archive libraries (i.e., the *lib*.a* files).

Another issue involving static libraries is the order in which things are listed when libraries are linked. The Darwin link editor loads object files and libraries in the exact order given in the *cc* command. As an example, suppose we've created a static archive library named *libmtr.a*. Consider the following attempt to link to this library:

```
cc -L. -lmtr -o testlibmtr testlibmtr.o
/usr/bin/ld: Undefined symbols:
_cot
_csc
_sec
make: *** [testlibmtr] Error 1
```

The rewrite of the command works as follows:

```
cc -o testlibmtr testlibmtr.o -L. -lmtr
```

In the first case, the library is placed first and no undefined symbols are encountered, so the library is ignored (there's nothing to be done with it). However, the second attempt is successful, because the object files are placed before the library. For the link editor to realize that it needs to look for undefined symbols (which are defined in the library), it must encounter the object files before the static library.

Prebinding

Whenever you install an update to the Mac OS X operating system, there is a long phase at the end called *optimization*. What the splash screen calls "optimization" is a particular type of optimization, called *prebinding*, which applies only to Mach-O executables. We will only describe the essential idea behind prebinding. For more details and specific instructions on building libraries and executables with prebinding enabled, consult the document */Developer/Documentation/ReleaseNotes/Prebinding.html*.

To understand what prebinding is and how it can speed up the launch of an application, let's consider what happens when you launch an application that was built without prebinding. When such an application (or dynamic library) is built, *ld* (the static linker) records the names of undefined symbols (i.e., the names of symbols that the application must link against).

Later, when the application is launched, the dynamic linker (*dyld*) must bind the undefined references from the application to their definitions.

In contrast, if an executable or dynamic library is built with prebinding, the binding essentially occurs at build time. In particular, the library is predefined at some specified address range, a process that would otherwise have to occur when an application is launched. Rather than mark symbols as undefined, the dynamic linker can use address symbols in a prebound library to reference when some other application or dynamic library links against it. Additionally, if the prebound library depends on other libraries (a common situation), then the static linker records the timestamps of the other libraries. Later, when the prebound library is used, the dynamic linker checks the timestamps of the dependent libraries and checks for the existence of overlapping executable addresses. If the timestamps do not match those of the build timestamps, or if there are overlapping executable addresses, the prebinding is broken and normal binding is performed.

Interesting and Important Libraries

Table 5-2 lists some significant libraries included with Mac OS X and Table 5-3 lists some significant libraries that *do not* come with Mac OS X (but are available through Fink).

Table 5-2. Important Mac OS X libraries

Library	Description	Headers
libalias	A packet aliasing library for masquerading and network address translation	Not included in Mac OS X. See the network_cmds module in the Darwin CVS archive.
libl.a	The *lex* runtime library	Not applicable. Lexical analyzers that you generate with *lex* have all the necessary definitions.
libMallocDebug	A library for the *MallocDebug* utility (*/Developer/ Applications*)	Not applicable. You don't need to do anything special with your code to use this utility.
libncurses (*libcurses* is available for backward compatibility.)	The new curses screen library, a set of functions for controlling a terminal's display screen	*/usr/include/ncurses.h* (*curses.h* is available for backward compatibility.)
libobjc	The library for the GNU Objective-C compiler	*/usr/include/objc/**
libpcap	Packet capture library	*/usr/include/pcap**
libssl and *libcrypto*	An OpenSSL: Open Source toolkit implementing the Secure Sockets Layer (SSL v2/v3) and Transport Layer Security (TLS v1) protocols, as well as a full-strength, general-purpose cryptography library	*/usr/include/openssl/**

Table 5-2. Important Mac OS X libraries (continued)

Library	Description	Headers
libtcl	The Tcl runtime library	*/usr/include/tcl.h*
liby.a	The *yacc* runtime library	Not applicable. Parsers that you generate with *yacc* have all the necessary definitions.
libz	A general-purpose data-compression library (*Zlib*)	*zlib.h*

Table 5-3. Libraries that are missing from Mac OS X

Fink package	Description	Home page
aalib	ASCII art library	*http://aa-project.sourceforge.net/aalib*
db3	Berkeley DB embedded database	*http://www.sleepycat.com/*
db4	Berkeley DB embedded database	*http://www.sleepycat.com/*
dlcompat	Dynamic loading compatibility library	*http://fink.sourceforge.net*
dtdparser	Java DTD Parser	*http://www.wutka.com/dtdparser.html*
expat	C library for parsing XML	*http://expat.sf.net*
fnlib	Font rendering library for X11	*http://www.enlightenment.org/*
freetype	TrueType font rendering library, version 1	*http://www.freetype.org/*
freetype2	TrueType font rendering library, version 2	*http://www.freetype.org/*
gc	General-purpose garbage collection library	*http://www.hpl.hp.com/personal/Hans_Boehm/gc/*
gd	Graphics generation library	*http://www.boutell.com/gd/*
gdal	Translator for raster geospatial data formats	*http://www.remotesensing.org/gdal/*
gdbm	GNU dbm	*http://www.gnu.org*
giflib	GIF image format handling library, LZW-enabled version	*http://prtr-13.ucsc.edu/~badger/software/libungif/*
glib	Low-level library that supports GTK+ and GNOME	*http://www.gtk.org/*
gmp	GNU multiple precision arithmetic library	*http://www.swox.com/gmp/*
gnomelibs	GNOME libraries	*http://www.gnome.org*
gnujaxp	Basic XML processing in Java	*http://www.gnu.org/software/classpathx/jaxp*
gtk	GTK+, the GIMP widget toolkit used by GNOME	*http://www.gtk.org/*
hermes	Optimized pixel format conversion library	*http://www.canlib.org/hermes/*
imlib	General image handling library	*http://www.enlightenment.org/pages/imlib2.html*
libdivxdecore	OpenDivX codec	*http://www.projectmayo.com/projects/detail.php?projectId=4*
libdnet	Networking library	*http://libdnet.sourceforge.net/*

Table 5-3. Libraries that are missing from Mac OS X (continued)

Fink package	Description	Home page
libdockapp	Library that eases the creation of Window-Maker Dock applets	*ftp://shadowmere.student.utwente.nl/pub/WindowMaker/*
libdv	Software decoder for DV format video	*http://www.sourceforge.net/projects/libdv/*
libfame	Fast Assembly Mpeg Encoding library	*http://fame.sourceforge.net/*
libghttp	HTTP client library	*http://www.gnome.org/*
libiconv	Character set conversion library	*http://clisp.cons.org/~haible/packages-libiconv.html*
libiodbc	ODBC libraries	*http://www.mysql.com/*
libjconv	Japanese code conversion library	*http://www.kondara.org/libjconv/index.html.en*
libjpeg	JPEG image format handling library	*http://www.ijg.org/*
libmpeg	GIMP MPEG library	*http://www.gimp.org*
libmusicbrainz	Client library for the MusicBrainz CD Index	*http://www.musicbrainz.org*
libnasl	Nessus Attack Scripting Language	*http://www.nessus.org/*
libnessus	Libraries package for Nessus without SSL support	*http://www.nessus.org/*
libole2	Library for the OLE2 compound file format	*http://www.gnome.org/*
libpoll	System V *poll(2)* Emulation Library	*http://fink.sourceforge.net*
libproplist	Routines for string list handling	*http://www.windowmaker.org/*
libshout	Library for streaming to icecast	*http://developer.icecast.org/libshout/*
libsigc++	Callback system for widget libraries	*http://developer.icecast.org/libshout/*
libstroke	Translates mouse strokes to program commands	*http://www.etla.net/libstroke/*
libtiff	TIFF image format library	*http://www.libtiff.org/*
libungif	GIF image format handling library, LZW-free version	*http://prtr-13.ucsc.edu/~badger/software/libungif/index.shtml*
libunicode	Low-level Unicode processing library	*http://www.sourceforge.net/projects/libunicode/*
libwww	General-purpose Web API written in C for Unix and Windows	*http://www.w3c.org/Library/Distribution.html*
libxml	XML parsing library	*http://www.gnome.org/*
libxml++	C++ interface to the *libxml2* XML parsing library	*http://sourceforge.net/projects/libxmlplusplus/*
libxml2	XML parsing library, version 2	*http://www.xmlsoft.org/*
libxpg4	Locale-enabling preload library	*http://www.darwinfo.org/devlist.php3?number=9143*
libxslt	XSLT library	*http://www.xmlsoft.org/XSLT/*

Table 5-3. Libraries that are missing from Mac OS X (continued)

Fink package	Description	Home page
log4j	Library that helps the programmer output log statements to a variety of output targets	*http://jakarta.apache.org/log4j*
lzo	Real-time data compression library	*http://www.oberhumer.com/opensource/lzo*
neon	HTTP/WebDAV client library with a C API	*http://www.webdav.org/neon/*
netpbm	Graphics manipulation programs and libraries	*http://netpbm.sourceforge.net*
pcre	Perl Compatible Regular Expressions library	*http://www.pcre.org*
pdflib	A library for generating PDFs	*http://www.pdflib.com/pdflib*
pil	The Python Imaging Library; adds image-processing capabilities to Python	*http://www.pythonware/products/pil*
pilot-link	Palm libraries	*http://www.pilot-link.org/*
popt	Library for parsing command-line options	*http://www.gnu.org/directory/popt.html*
pth	Portable library that provides scheduling	*http://www.gnu.org/software/pth/pth.html*
readline	Terminal input library	*http://cnswww.cns.cwru.edu/~chet/readline/rltop.html*
slang	Embeddable extension language and console I/O library	*http://space.mit.edu/~davis/slang/*
stlport	ANSI C++ Standard Library implementation	*http://www.stlport.org/*

The list of available libraries is ever-growing, thanks to an influx of open source ports from FreeBSD and Linux. One of the best ways to keep on top of the latest ports is to install Fink (see the "Fink" section in Chapter 6), which lets you install precompiled versions of libraries and applications or install them from source.

CHAPTER 6
Creating and Installing Packages

Just because you can build all your applications from source doesn't mean that you should. Linux users are spoiled by the wealth of applications that they can download as Red Hat or Debian packages. FreeBSD users have the best of both worlds (packaged software and building from source) through the vast number of applications in */usr/ports*. Mac OS X users can tap into this wealth of applications through the Fink and GNU-Darwin projects.

However, if you go through the trouble of building applications from source, you might want to package the resulting binaries for distribution so others can install the package, you can reinstall it at a later time without needing to rebuild it from source, or you can install it on multiple machines. Mac OS X is quite rich in the number of options available for packaging.

This chapter covers the Fink and GNU-Darwin distributions, as well as the packaging tools that come with Mac OS X's Developer Tools, and shows you how to package your application for distribution.

Fink

Christoph Pfisterer* started the Fink project in December 2000. A number of other people continued the project after Pfisterer left it in 2002.

Fink is essentially a port of the Debian Advanced Package Tool (APT), with some frontends and its own centralized collection site, which stores packaged binaries, source code, and patches needed to build software on Mac OS X. The Fink package manager allows you to install a package, choosing whether to install it from source or a binary package. Consistent with

---

* Pfisterer named the project Fink, the German word for finch, while thinking about Charles Darwin's study of finches on the Galapagos Islands.

Debian, binary package files are in the *dpkg* format with a *.deb* extension and are managed with the ported Debian tools *dpkg* and *apt-get*.

Fink also provides new tools that create a *.deb* package from source. A database of installed software is maintained that identifies packages by the combination of name, version, and revision. Moreover, Fink understands dependencies, uses CVS to propagate software updates, supports uninstallation, and makes it easy to see available packages and installed packages. Fink can be used to install XFree86, as well as several hundred other popular Unix packages. If you already have a copy of XFree86 installed, Fink recognizes and supports it.

Although Fink does not manage Mac OS X packages, it does require Mac OS X Developer Tools.

Fink installs itself and all of its packages, with the exception of XFree86, in a directory named */sw*, thus completely separating it from the main system directory */usr*. A more traditional Unix practice is to place locally installed software in */usr/local*. Installing software in */sw* takes the usual practice one step further and is regarded as a safer policy. If problems occur with Fink-installed packages, you can then delete the entire */sw* directory tree without affecting your system.

You can install Fink from binary or source. Both methods of installation are simple. The binary installation involves the following steps:

1. Download the binary installer disk image (a *.dmg* file) from *http://fink. sourceforge.net/download*.

2. In the Finder, double-click the *.dmg* file to mount the disk image.

3. Open the mounted disk image and double-click the Fink Installer *.pkg* package inside.

4. Follow the instructions on the screen.

To install Fink from source, perform the following steps.

1. Download the source tarball from *http://fink.sourceforge.net/download/ srcdist.php* to a temporary directory using the command line. For example:

```
cd /tmp
curl -O http://prdownloads.sourceforge.net/fink/fink-0.4.0a-full.tar.gz
```

Do not use StuffIt to unpack the tarball, as it will corrupt some files; you should unpack the tarball from the command line. Also, check the Fink site for the latest release.

2. Issue the command *gnutar -xzf fink-0.4.0a-full.tar.gz*. This creates a directory with the same name as the archive, e.g., *fink-0.4.0a-full/*.

3. Change into that directory and run the *bootstrap* script:

```
cd fink-0.4.0a-full
./bootstrap.sh
```

4. Follow the instructions on the screen.

To begin using Fink, you need to set up your PATH and some environment variables. Fink provides shell scripts to help with this. If you are using *tcsh* or *csh*, you can execute this command before using Fink applications (or add it to your *.cshrc* or *.tcshrc* file, depending on which one you have):

```
source /sw/bin/init.csh
```

If you are using *sh*, *zsh*, *ksh*, or *bash*, you can run this command (or add it to your *.profile* or *.bash_profile* file):

```
. /sw/bin/init.sh
```

Use the following command to perform additional post-install configuration (you will be prompted for your password):

```
fink scanpackages
```

Fink can later be updated by entering the commands:

```
fink selfupdate
fink update-all
```

The first command updates Fink itself, including the list and descriptions of available packages, while the second command updates any installed packages. Once Fink has been installed, you can see what packages are available by entering the command *fink list*.

You can download and install binaries via *dselect* (shown in Figure 6-1), a console-based frontend to *dpkg*. To use *dselect*, you need to have superuser (or administrator) privileges, so you'll need to run *sudo dselect* in the Terminal. Once *dselect* has started, you can use the following options to maintain, install, and uninstall packages:

[A]ccess

Chooses the access method to use. Configures the network access method to use.

[U]pdate

Downloads the list of available packages from the Fink site. This option is equivalent to running *apt-get update*. Table 6-1 lists the *apt-get* and *dpkg* command-line options.

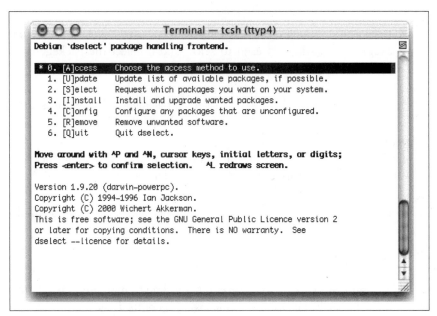

```
●  ●  ●                    Terminal — tcsh (ttyp4)
Debian `dselect' package handling frontend.

* 0. [A]ccess    Choose the access method to use.
  1. [U]pdate    Update list of available packages, if possible.
  2. [S]elect    Request which packages you want on your system.
  3. [I]nstall   Install and upgrade wanted packages.
  4. [C]onfig    Configure any packages that are unconfigured.
  5. [R]emove    Remove unwanted software.
  6. [Q]uit      Quit dselect.

Move around with ^P and ^N, cursor keys, initial letters, or digits;
Press <enter> to confirm selection.   ^L redraws screen.

Version 1.9.20 (darwin-powerpc).
Copyright (C) 1994-1996 Ian Jackson.
Copyright (C) 2000 Wichert Akkerman.
This is free software; see the GNU General Public Licence version 2
or later for copying conditions.  There is NO warranty.  See
dselect --licence for details.
```

Figure 6-1. The dselect program's main menu

Table 6-1. Some apt-get and dpkg commands

Command	Description
apt-get update	Updates list of available packages. Do this first.
apt-get install *foo*	Downloads and installs package *foo*.
apt-get remove *foo*	Deletes package *foo*.
dpkg --list	Lists all installed packages.
dpkg --listfiles *foo*	Lists all the files from package *foo*.
dpkg --install *foo*	Installs package *foo*.
dpkg --remove *foo*	Deletes package *foo*. Leaves configuration files.
dpkg --purge *foo*	Deletes *foo* and configuration files.
dpkg -S */path/to/file*	Tells you which package owns a file.

 You must run *[U]pdate* at least once after installing Fink.

[S]elect

Requests the packages you want on your system. Displays the actual package listing, which is used to select and deselect the packages you want on your system.

[I]nstall

Installs, upgrades, and configures selected packages. Also removes deselected packages.

[C]onfig

Configures any packages that are unconfigured. Not actually needed, since [I]nstall does this after you've installed a package.

[R]emove

Removes unwanted software. Not actually needed, since [I]nstall will do this.

[Q]uit

Quits deselect.

The *fink* command is used from the command line to maintain, install, and uninstall packages. Table 6-2 lists some examples of its usage.

Table 6-2. Various fink commands

Command	Description
fink selfupdate	Updates Fink along with package list. Do this first.
fink update-all	Updates all installed packages.
fink install *foo*	Downloads source, then builds and installs Debian package *foo*.
fink reinstall *foo*	Reinstalls *foo* using *dpkg*.
fink describe *foo*	Describes package *foo*.
fink list	Lists available packages. "i" is placed next to installed packages.
fink build *foo*	Downloads and builds Debian package *foo*. No installation is performed.
fink rebuild *foo*	Downloads and rebuilds Debian package *foo*. Installation is performed.
fink --remove *foo*	Deletes package *foo*, ignoring dependencies. Use *apt-get remove* instead.

Using Fink, you can mix binary and source installations. That is, you can install some packages from their precompiled *.deb* files and others from source. If you do this, you will need to first use *apt-get* to update the available binaries and subsequently use *fink selfupdate*, followed by *fink update-all*, to update packages installed from source.

Creating Fink Packages

You can create your own Fink packages by identifying a source archive and creating a *.info* file in your */sw/fink/dists/local/main/finkinfo* directory.

Sample Program

To demonstrate how to create a package, we'll create a short C program and its associated manpage. Example 6-1 shows *hellow.c* and Example 6-2 shows its manpage, *hellow.1*.

Example 6-1. The Hello, World sample program

```
/*
 * hellow.c - Prints a friendly greeting.
 */

#include <stdio.h>

int main( )
{
  printf("Hello, world!\n");
  return 0;
}
```

Example 6-2. The manpage for hellow.c

```
.\" Copyright (c) 2002, O'Reilly & Associates, Inc.
.\"
.Dd April 15, 2002
.Dt HELLOW 1
.Os Mac OS X
.Sh NAME
.Nm hellow
.Nd Greeting generator
.Sh DESCRIPTION
This command prints a friendly greeting.
```

Creating and Publishing the Tarball

The Fink package system needs a tarball that can be downloaded with the *curl* utility, so you should put these two files into a directory, such as *hellow-1.0*. Then, create a tarball containing these files and that top-level directory, and put it somewhere where you can get it. In this example, the tarball is created and moved to the local *Shared* folder:

```
[localhost:~/src] bjepson% tar cvfz hellow-1.0.tar.gz hellow-1.0/
hellow-1.0/
hellow-1.0/hellow.1
hellow-1.0/hellow.c
hellow-1.0/Makefile
[localhost:~/src] bjepson% cp hellow-1.0.tar.gz /Users/Shared
```

The *curl* utility can download this file with the following URL: *file:///Users/ Shared/hellow-1.0.tar.gz*. (We could also have put the file on a public web server or FTP server.)

Creating the .info File

Next, you need a *.info* file to tell Fink where to download the package and how to install it. Fink can use this information to download, extract, and compile the source code, and then generate and install a Debian package (*.deb* file). To create the file in */sw/fink/dists/local/main/finkinfo*, you'll need superuser privileges (use the *sudo* utility to temporarily gain these privileges). Example 6-3 shows *hellow-1.0.info*.

Example 6-3. The hellow-1.0 info file

```
Package: hellow
Version: 1.0
Revision: 1
Source: file:///Users/Shared/%n-%v.tar.gz
CompileScript: make
InstallScript: mkdir -p %i/bin
 cp %n %i/bin
 mkdir -p %i/share/man/man1
 cp %n.1 %i/share/man/man1/%n.1
Description: Hello, World program
DescDetail: <<
Prints a friendly greeting to you and your friends.
<<
License: Public Domain
Maintainer: Brian Jepson <bjepson@oreilly.com>
```

The *hellow-1.0.info* file includes several entries, described in the following list. See the Fink Packaging Manual on *http://fink.sourceforge.net/doc/ packaging/* for more details.

Package
    The name of the package.

Version
    The package version.

Revision

The package revision number.

Source

The URL of the source distribution. You can use percent expansion in the name. (In this example, %n is the name of the package and %v is the package version.) See the Fink Packaging Manual for more percent expansions.

CompileScript

The command (or commands) needed to compile the source package. The command(s) may span multiple lines, but must begin after the colon.

InstallScript

The command (or commands) that install the compiled package. The command(s) may span multiple lines, but must begin after the colon.

Description

A short description of the package.

DescDetail

A longer description of the package, enclosed with << >>.

License

The license used by the package. See the Fink Packaging Manual for information on available licenses.

Maintainer

The name and email address of the maintainer.

Installing the Package

To install *hellow*, use the command *sudo fink install hellow*. This command downloads the source to a working directory, and then extracts, compiles, and packages it, generating the file */sw/fink/dists/local/main/binary-darwin-powerpc/hellow_1.0-1_darwin-powerpc.deb*. After fink creates this file, it installs it using *dpkg*. After you've installed *hellow*, you can view its manpage and run the *hellow* command:

```
% man hellow

HELLOW(1)        System General Commands Manual        HELLOW(1)

NAME
     hellow - Greeting generator

DESCRIPTION
     This command prints a friendly greeting.
```

```
% hellow
Hello, world!
```

This example shows only a portion of Fink's capabilities. For example, Fink can download and apply patches to a source distribution. For more information, see the Fink Packaging Manual, which contains detailed instructions on how to build and contribute a *.deb* package to the Fink distribution.

GNU-Darwin

The FreeBSD ports and package management system is used by the GNU-Darwin distribution (*http://gnu-darwin.sourceforge.net*).

The ports system provides for packaging an application as a single file that contains precompiled binaries, as well as associated configuration and documentation files. Like *dpkg*, this system allows the installation of a software package with a single command. This system also maintains an installed package database and understands dependencies. Additionally, to support installing remote packages, a remote ports tree is established. The ports tree resides on your computer and includes makefiles that know how to find, patch, compile, package, and install software packages from source code. Current versions of ported software are stored in one or more ports trees.

 Unlike Fink, GNU-Darwin does not restrict itself to one portion of your filesystem, and it will make changes to system binaries. We suggest that you read the *one_stop* script carefully before you execute it.

To install GNU-Darwin, perform the following steps:

1. Download the *one_stop* script from *http://gnu-darwin.sourceforge.net/ one_stop*.

2. Read the *one_stop* script so you know what it's going to do.

3. Execute the *one_stop* script as *root* (*sudo csh one_stop*).

The *one_stop* installer downloads and installs many packages, so give it some time to complete.

 The *one_stop* installer requires a considerable amount of bandwidth and does not allow you to choose a subset of packages, so it should not be attempted on a low-bandwidth connection. Again, read the script before you run it. As of this writing, the script states that GNU-Darwin will take up one gigabyte of disk space when *one_stop* finishes.

After you install GNU-Darwin, you can install additional software by downloading precompiled tarballs and using the package management commands listed in Table 6-3. Alternatively, you can install the GNU-Darwin ports system from *http://gnu-darwin.sourceforge.net/ports/* and then:

1. *cd* to */usr/ports.*
2. Find the subdirectory of the port you want to install and *cd* into it.
3. Run the command *sudo make install*, which performs the following:
   a. Downloads the source code for the package.
   b. Downloads and applies any relevant patches.
   c. Compiles and installs the package.
   d. Repeats those steps for any dependencies.

After you install the package with *make install*, you can manage it with the package management tools shown in Table 6-3.

Table 6-3. Using the FreeBSD package management system

Command	Description
pkg_add *package.tgz*	Adds (installs) a *package*.
pkg_add -r *package.tgz*	Adds a remote *package*. Checks a predetermined ports tree location.
pkg_delete *package*	Deletes (uninstalls) a *package*.
pkg_info	Shows information on installed *packages*.
pkg_info *package*	Shows information on an installed *package*.
pkg_info -L *package*	Shows files belonging to a *package*.
pkg_version	Compares versions of installed *packages* with current versions in ports tree.

Packaging Tools

The following packaging options come with Mac OS X.

PackageMaker
> Found in */Developer/Applications*, PackageMaker can be used to create packages that are bundles consisting of all the items that the Mac OS X Installer (*/Applications/Utilities*) needs to perform an installation. PackageMaker can also create metapackages, which can be used to install multiple packages at the same time.

gnutar and gzip
> The Unix tape archive tools (*tar* and *gnutar*; *gnutar* is preferred because it can handle longer pathnames) are used to bundle the directories and

resources for distribution. GNU Zip (*gzip*) is used to compress the tar archives to make file sizes as small as possible. Using these tools is generally the simplest way to copy a collection of files from one machine to another.

Disk Copy

One of the easiest ways to distribute an application is to use Disk Copy (*/Applications/Utilities*) to create a disk image. You can use Disk Copy to create a double-clickable archive, which mounts as a disk image on the user's desktop. From there, the user can choose to mount the disk image each time the application is run, copy the application to the hard drive (usually to the */Applications* directory), or burn the image to a CD.

Each of these tools will be discussed separately in the sections that follow.

Using PackageMaker

Apple's native format for packaging and distributing software is Package-Maker. Packages created with PackageMaker have a *.pkg* extension. When a user double-clicks on a package, the Installer application (*/Applications/Utilities*) is invoked and the installation process begins. These packages are bundles that contain all of the items the Installer needs.

You can also use PackageMaker to create *metapackages* for installing multiple packages. Metapackages, or bundles, contain meta-information, files, and libraries associated with a given application. Packages can also contain multiple versions of an application; typically, both Mac OS X and Classic versions.

PackageMaker documentation is available in the Help Viewer at */Developer/Documentation/DeveloperTools/PackageMaker/PackageMaker.help*.

The basic components of a package are:

- A bill of materials (*.bom*) binary file that describes the contents of the package. You can view the contents of a bill of materials with the *lsbom* command.

- An information file (*.info*) that contains the information entered in the GUI application PackageMaker when the package was created.

- An archive file (*.pax*) that contains the complete set of files to be installed by the package. (This archive file can be compressed, giving it a *.pax.gz* extension.) This is similar to a *tar* archive.

- A size calculation file (*.sizes*) that lists the sizes of the compressed and uncompressed software.

- Resources that the installer uses during the installation, such as *README* files, license agreements, and pre- and post-install scripts. These resources are typically not installed; instead, they are used only during the installation process.

Setting up the directory

To demonstrate how to create a package, we'll use the *hellow.c* and *hellow.1* examples shown earlier in this chapter (in Example 6-1 and Example 6-2).

PackageMaker expects you to set up the files using a directory structure that mirrors your intended installation. So, if you plan to install *hellow* into */usr/bin*, and *hellow.1* into */usr/share/man/man1*, you'll need to create the appropriate subdirectories under your working directory.

Suppose that your *hellow* project resides in *~/src/hellow*. To keep things organized, you can create a subdirectory called *stage* that contains the installation directory. In that case, you'd want to place the *hellow* binary in *~/src/hellow/stage/bin* and the *hellow.1* manpage in *~/src/hellow/stage/share/man/man1*. The makefile shown in Example 6-4 compiles *hellow.c*, creates the *stage* directory and its subdirectories, and copies the distribution files into those directories when you run the command *make prep*.

Example 6-4. makefile for hellow

```
hellow:
        cc -o hellow hellow.c

prep: hellow
        mkdir -p stage/bin
        mkdir -p stage/share/man/man1
        cp hellow stage/bin/
        cp hellow.1 stage/share/man/man1/
```

> The directories you create in the *stage* directory should have the same permissions as the directories into which you are installing the package. If your *umask* is set so that the permissions are not right, use *chmod* in your makefile to correct the permissions after you create the staging directories.

To get started, you need only *hellow.c*, *hellow.1*, and *makefile*. When you run the command *make prep*, it compiles the program and copies the files to their locations in the *stage* directory. After that, you're ready to launch PackageMaker and bundle up the application.

Creating the package

Run PackageMaker and set the options as appropriate for your package. Figure 6-2 through Figure 6-6 show the settings for the *hellow* sample. The options are as follows:

Description tab
   Contains items that describe the package so the person installing the package can find its name and version.

   Title
      The title, or name, of the package.

   Version
      The version number of the package.

   Description
      A description of the package.

   Delete Warning
      A custom warning message to display when a user removes the package. Mac OS X does not have a utility to uninstall a package, though.

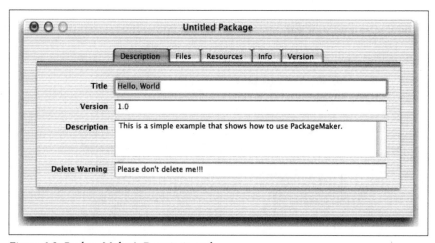

Figure 6-2. PackageMaker's Description tab

Files tab

Contains information related to file locations and compression.

Root

This option indicates where PackageMaker can find the top-level staging directory.

Compress Archive

You should leave this option enabled, since it makes the package smaller.

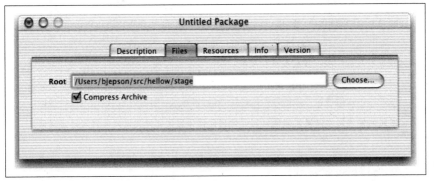

Figure 6-3. PackageMaker's Files tab

Resources tab

Specifies the location of extra resources.

Resources

The Resources directory contains files, such as *README* files, that are used by the installer but aren't installed on the disk. See PackageMaker help for details.

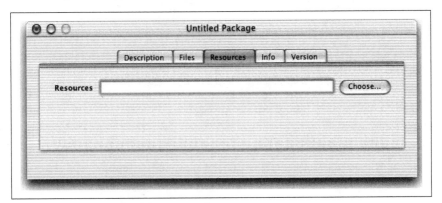

Figure 6-4. PackageMaker's Resources tab

Info tab

Specifies miscellaneous package options.

Default Location

This option indicates the default target location for the package.

Restart Action

If this option is set to Required Restart, the system must be rebooted when the installation is finished. Other options include No Restart Required, Recommended Restart, and Shutdown Required.

Authorization Action

Set this option to Root Authorization if the user needs to supply authentication to install the package. (This escalates the user's privileges to *root* temporarily.) Other options include No Authorization Required and Admin Authorization (if the user needs only to *be* an Admin user, but does not need to escalate privileges). If the package will be installed into a protected directory (such as */usr*), you should use Root Authorization.

Allows Back Rev.

This option allows the user to install an older version of the package over a newer one.

Install Fat

This option supports multiple architecture binaries.

Relocatable

This option allows the user to choose an alternate location for the installed files.

Required

This option implies that certain packages (when installed as part of a larger install) are required.

Root Volume Only

This option requires that the user install the package on the current root volume (the volume from which you booted Mac OS X).

Update Installed Languages Only

When you update a package, this option will only update the currently installed localization projects.

Overwrite Permissions

If the installer overwrites an existing file or directory, this option will cause it to change the permissions to match what Package-Maker found in the staging area.

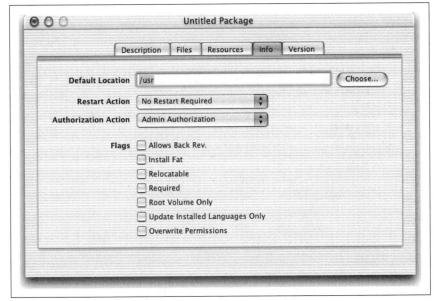

Figure 6-5. PackageMaker's Info tab

Version tab

Specifies detailed version information.

Display name

The name of the package to use when reporting its version

Identifier

A unique package name

Get-Info string

The version number to use when inspecting the package in the Finder with Get Info

Short version

An abbreviated version number

Version: Major

A major version number (the *1* in 1.0)

Version: Minor

A minor version number (the *0* in 1.0)

After you have filled in the package settings, select Tools → Create Package to create the *.pkg* file. To install it, double-click on the file and install as you would any other Mac OS X package.

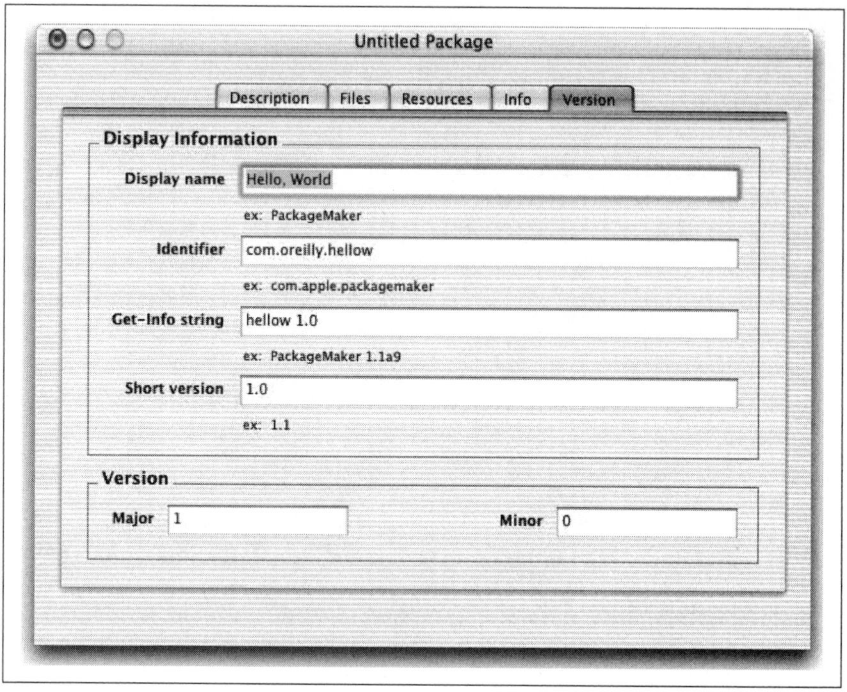

Figure 6-6. PackageMaker's Version tab

Using GNU tar

For Unix-based software that does not involve resource forks or creator types, *gnutar* and *gzip* can be used to create a *.tar.gz* or *.tgz* tarball. This type of tarball preserves paths, permissions, and symbolic links. It also supports authentication and compresses well. Tools to uncompress the tarball are available for many platforms.

The automated creation of such a tarball can be worked into the same *makefile* that is used to build the software. Preservation of resource forks is tricky, but possible, in this method. For example, the following command preserves Macintosh resource forks (where *foo/* is a directory):

```
gnutar -pczf foo.tgz foo/
```

Every good tarball has a single top-level directory that contains everything else. You should not create tarballs that dump their contents into the current directory. To install software packaged this way, you can use the following command:

```
gnutar -pxzf foo.tgz
```

This simply unpacks the tarball into the file and directory structure that existed prior to packaging. Basically, it reverses the packing step. This method can be used to simply write files to the appropriate places on the system, such as */usr/local/bin*, */usr/local/lib*, */usr/local/man*, */usr/local/include*, and so on.

 When creating packages, you should keep your package contents out of directories such as */etc*, */usr/bin*, */usr/lib*, */usr/include*, or any top-level directory reserved for the operating system, since you have no way of knowing what a future software update or Mac OS X upgrade will include. For example, the Fink project stays out of Mac OS X's way by keeping most of its files in */sw*. We suggest that you use */usr/local* for the packages that you compile.

This packaging method can also be arranged so that the unpacking is done first in a temporary directory. The user can then run an install script that relocates the package contents to their final destination. This approach is usually preferred, since the *install* script could be designed to do some basic checking of dependencies, the existence of destination directories, the recataloging of libraries, etc. You could also include an *uninstall* script with your distribution.

The disadvantages of the tarball method of distributing software are:

- There is no built-in mechanism for keeping track of which files go where.
- There is no built-in method for uninstalling the software.
- It is difficult to list what software is installed and how the installed files depend on each other or on other libraries.
- There is no checking of dependencies and prerequisite software prior to the installation.

These tasks could be built into *install* and *uninstall* scripts, but there is no inherently uniform, consistent, and coherent method for accomplishing these tasks when multiple software packages are installed in this manner. Fortunately, more sophisticated methods of packaging, distributing, and maintaining software on Unix systems have been devised, such as Red Hat's RPM, Debian's *dpkg*, and Apple's PackageMaker.

Disk Images

Many applications in Mac OS X do not require a special installer. Often, they can be installed by simply dragging the application's folder or icon to a convenient location in the directory structure, usually the */Applications* folder. Applications that are distributed this way are typically packaged as a *disk image*. A disk image is a file that, when double-clicked, creates a virtual volume that is mounted on the user's desktop, as shown in Figure 6-7.

Inside Applications

Actually, an application *is* a folder with the extension *.app*, which is typically hidden from the user. This folder contains all of the application's resources. To view the contents of an application bundle, Control-click on the application icon and select Show Package Contents from the pop-up menu. This will open the application's *Contents* folder in the Finder.

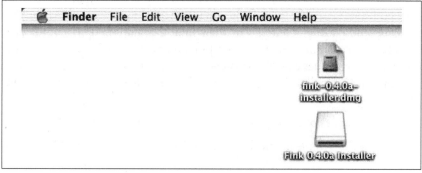

Figure 6-7. A disk image and its mounted volume

 You can turn a Java application into a *.app* with *MRJApp-Builder* (*/Developer/Applications*). Since Mac OS X comes with Java, you can place your Java application on a disk image, secure in the knowledge that any Mac OS X user can double-click on the application to launch it.

Disk images can be created either using Disk Copy (*/Applications/Utilities*) or via the command line (described later). There are two types of disk images. One is a *dual fork* disk image with an *.img* extension, and the other is a *single fork* disk image with a *.dmg* extension. A dual fork disk image requires additional (MacBinary) encoding in order for it to be transferred across networks. The single fork version is preferred for distributing software in Mac OS X, as it requires no additional encoding.

The Unix command *df* will reveal a disk image as a mounted volume, and it will appear in the */Volumes* directory. When you are done with the mounted volume, it can be ejected to unmount it. This is accomplished by clicking on the volume (in Figure 6-7, the mounted volume is named Fink 0.4.0a Installer) to select it and going to File → Eject (⌘-E). You could also drag the mounted volume to the Trash.

> If you've used earlier versions of the Mac OS, you're probably familiar with the Put Away command (⌘-Y); however, that command no longer exists for Mac OS X. Instead, you must use Eject to unmount a disk image.

Creating a disk image with Disk Copy

To create a disk image using Disk Copy, perform the following steps:

1. Launch Disk Copy (*/Applications/Utilities*).
2. Select File → New → Blank Image. Disk Copy prompts you for a name, location, size (the maximum size is limited by available disk space), volume name, format, and encryption options, as shown in Figure 6-8. If you choose to enable encryption, Disk Copy will prompt you for a passphrase.

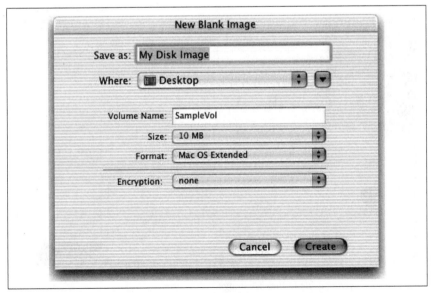

Figure 6-8. Creating a new blank image with Disk Copy

3. Name the new image "My Disk Image" and choose the Desktop as the location. Set the Volume Name to "SampleVol" and click Create. The new image will be created as *My Disk Image.dmg* and mounted as SampleVol.

4. Double-click on the disk icon to open the empty volume in a Finder window, as shown in Figure 6-9.

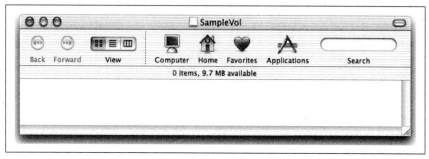

Figure 6-9. A blank disk image, ready to be loaded up with files

5. Select File → New Finder Window (or ⌘-N) to open a new Finder window, where you can select the files you want to place in the disk image, as shown in Figure 6-10.

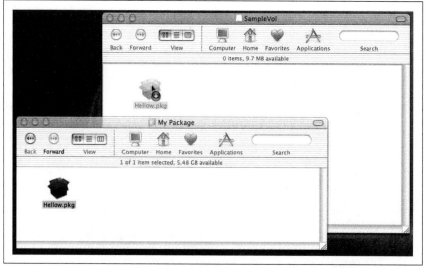

Figure 6-10. Copying a file to the disk image

6. To copy the files to the mounted volume, select and then drag the items into the empty SampleVol window.

7. Once you've placed the files into the disk image, eject this disk (⌘-E, or drag SampleVol to the Trash).

8. Return to the Disk Copy application, select File → Convert Image, locate the disk image file in the Convert Image window, and click on the Convert button, as shown in Figure 6-11.

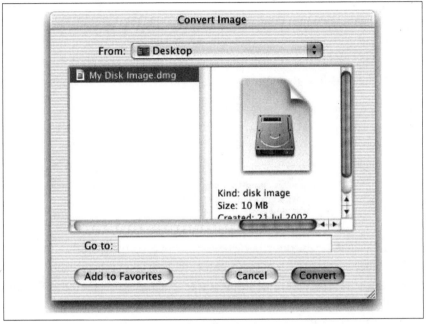

Figure 6-11. Choosing the image to convert

9. The Convert Image window will change. Enter either a new name or the same name in the Save As field, and then select read-only from the Image Format pull-down menu, as shown in Figure 6-12. (You can also compress the disk image from this selection.)

10. Click the Convert button. If you've given the disk image the same file-name as the original image you created, an alert window will appear, asking you to confirm whether or not you want to replace the older file with the new one. Click Replace to finish the process.

11. Quit Disk Copy (⌘-Q).

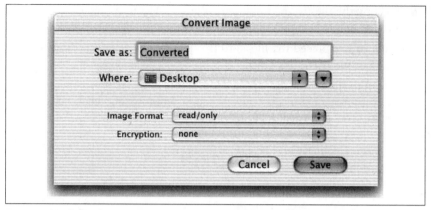

Figure 6-12. Converting an image

Creating a disk image from the command line

The following example illustrates how to create a disk image at the command line.

> To avoid accidentally wiping out a physical disk, make sure you are logged in as an unprivileged user when you use these commands. Do not log in as *root* or use *sudo*.

1. Change (*cd*) to the directory where you want to create the disk image:

   ```
   cd ~/Documents
   ```

2. Create the disk image of a given size (10 MB in this example) using *hdiutil*:

   ```
   hdiutil create -megabytes 10 Sample.dmg -layout NONE
   ```

3. Associate the disk image with a device without actually mounting it:

   ```
   hdid -nomount Sample.dmg
   ```

   This attaches the image to the system under an unused device, such as */dev/disk2*. (*hdid* will report the device, or you can use *hdiutil info* to see all of the attached images.)

4. Format the disk as HFS+ with *newfs_hfs*. (Replace REAL_DEVICE with the actual device used, such as */dev/disk2*.) Be careful with this command—if you run it on your hard drive, it could wipe out your disk.

   ```
   newfs_hfs -v SampleVol /dev/REAL_DEVICE
   ```

5. Detach the newly formatted device:

   ```
   hdiutil eject /dev/REAL_DEVICE
   ```

6. Mount the writable image as a volume. Since you named it SampleVol when you issued the *newfs_hfs* command, it will appear on the desktop as SampleVol:

```
hdid Sample.dmg
```

7. Use the Finder or command-line tools to write to the volume SampleVol. It will appear on your desktop and will be available in */Volumes/SampleVol*.

8. When you are done writing to the volume, you can eject it in the Finder, using one of the methods described earlier.

9. Copy the disk image to a compressed, read-only image named *Ready4Dist.dmg*:

```
hdiutil convert -format UDZO Sample.dmg -o Ready4Dist.dmg
```

Whenever you want to mount this volume again, you can double-click the file *Ready4Dist.dmg* in the finder. Note that the writable disk image *Sample.dmg* is not destroyed in this process.

There were several names involved with that last example, so here's a refresher:

Sample.dmg
    A writable 10 MB disk image created in Step 2.

/dev/disk2, /dev/REAL_DEVICE
    The system device under which you attached *Sample.dmg* in Step 3.

SampleVol
    The volume name you gave to the disk image when you formatted this in Step 4.

Ready4Dist.dmg
    A read-only, compressed copy of *Sample.dmg*, created in Step 9. Since it's a copy, it has the same volume name as *Sample.dmg*: SampleVol.

Distributing Your Image

Once you've created a disk image, you can share it with the world. Put the image up on a web server or FTP server for others to enjoy, share it on your iDisk, or burn it to a CD using Disk Copy (select File → Burn Image).

## PART III

Beyond the User Space

This part of the book talks about the Darwin kernel, useful system administration tools, and how to set up the X Window System to work alongside Aqua. Chapters in this part include:

- Chapter 7, *Building the Darwin Kernel*
- Chapter 8, *System Management Tools*
- Chapter 9, *The X Window System*

Building the Darwin Kernel

The Darwin kernel, on which Mac OS X is based, is available in a publicly accessible CVS archive. This is not a watered-down version: you can rebuild a kernel that matches your current Mac OS X kernel in every respect. The only noticeable difference will be when you type *uname -v*:

```
Darwin Kernel Version 6.0: Sat Jul 27 13:18:52 PDT 2002;
root:xnu/xnu-344.obj~1/RELEASE_PPC
```

Just because you can build your kernel, does that mean you should? For most users, the answer is *no*, for the following reasons:

- For many users, configuring a Unix kernel involves little more than choosing and configuring device drivers. On Darwin, most devices are not in the kernel; they have their own top-level directory in the CVS archive. So, you do not need to configure Darwin to set up additional hardware support.

- Apple hardware is predictable. Most of you will be building Darwin for a G3 or G4 machine, and the range of possible chipsets is limited.

However, if you want to try installing an unofficial kernel patch, or if you want to try your hand at optimizing the kernel, then this chapter's for you.

Darwin Development Tools

The Darwin kernel requires a collection of development tools that are not part of the Mac OS X Developer Tools package. To get these tools, visit the Darwin project at *http://developer.apple.com/darwin/* and follow the links for the Darwin Development Environment for Mac OS X. Those links lead to a package called *darwintools.pkg*, which you should install. This package installs a number of header files, libraries, and tools into */usr/local*. The tools

A Safety Net

If you have enough disk space to install two copies of Mac OS X, please do so before you start playing around with your working kernel. That way, you will have an operating system you can boot into if things go bad. (On most G3 and G4 Macintoshes, you can hold down the Option key when booting to select a boot disk.) Most importantly, your spare install of Mac OS X will contain backups of important files, such as the kernel and critical frameworks. If you're low on disk space, why not treat yourself to a FireWire drive? If you have a newer Macintosh with a built-in FireWire port, you can boot from a Mac OS X-compatible FireWire drive.

are described in Table 7-1. The source code for these utilities and libraries can be found in the *cctools*, *mkisofs*, *Libstreams*, and *bootstrap_cmds* CVS modules. If you are working with an interim or seed release of Darwin or Mac OS X that is out of sync with the current Darwin Development Environment, you may need to check these utilities out and install them yourself.

Table 7-1. Darwin development tools

Tool	Description	CVS module
check_dylib	Checks the integrity of a dynamic library.	cctools
checksyms	Checks a binary to ensure that it adheres to Mac OS X conventions.	cctools
cmpshlib	Compares two versions of a shared library for compatibility.	cctools
decomment	Strips C and C++ comments from an input file.	bootstrap_cmds
devdump	Interactively reads the contents of a device or filesystem image.	mkisofs (as dump.c)
hack_libgcc	Hacks a framework to export backward-compatible symbols.	cctools
indr	Prepends an underscore to selected symbol names in an object file.	cctools
isodump	Interactively reads the contents of an ISO 9660 image.	mkisofs
isoinfo	Reads information from an ISO 9660 image. Use *isoinfo -h* for a usage summary.	mkisofs
isovfy	Verifies an ISO image.	mkisofs
kern_tool	Supports cross-compilation of the kernel; a hacked version of the *nm* utility.	cctools
mkhybrid	Creates a hybrid ISO 9660/Joliet/HFS filesystem.	mkisofs
mkisofs	Creates a hard link to *mkhybrid*.	mkisofs
mkshlib	Creates a host and target shared library. The host shared library looks like a static library to the linker, but at runtime, the target shared library is loaded.	cctools
relpath	Finds and prints a relative pathname, given a starting directory and an ending directory.	bootstrap_cmds

Table 7-1. Darwin development tools (continued)

Tool	Description	CVS module
seg_addr_table	Works with segment address tables.	cctools
seg_hack	Changes segment names.	cctools
setdbg	Operates as an interactive kernel debugger.	at_cmds

Getting the Source Code

To get the Darwin source code, you'll need to register with the Apple Open Source web site and check the source code out of the CVS archive. (The kernel source code weighs in at about 35 MB; after you compile the kernel, it will occupy about 150 MB.) To register for CVS access, visit *http://developer. apple.com/darwin/tools/cvs/*. That page should lead to a getting-started page, where you can register as a user.

The first step in registering is to agree to the Apple Public Source License (*http://www.opensource.apple.com/apsl/*). When you agree to that license, you can create a username and password that lets you check files out of CVS and view the web-based CVS archive.

Using CVS

When you register with Apple, you choose a username and password. You'll need to use that username and password when you log into CVS. The first step is setting your CVSROOT environment variable. Under *tcsh*, issue this command:

```
setenv CVSROOT :pserver:username@anoncvs.opensource.apple.com:/cvs/Darwin
```

Under *bash* or *zsh*, use this command:

```
export CVSROOT=:pserver:username@anoncvs.opensource.apple.com:/cvs/Darwin
```

Replace *username* with your username. After you set this environment variable, you can log into CVS with *cvs login*:

```
% cvs login
(Logging in to username@anoncvs.opensource.apple.com)
CVS password: ********
```

Checking out sources

To check out the source code for a module, use the *checkout* command:

```
cvs -z3 checkout [-r VERSION] modulename
```

The -z3 option tells CVS to use compression when transferring files.

Updating sources

To bring a module into sync with the latest changes to the repository, use the *update* command:

```
cvs -z3 update -P -d modulename
```

The *-d* option tells CVS to pick up any directories that were recently added, and *-P* tells CVS to prune any directories that were recently removed.

 If you use *modulename* with the *update* command, you need to be in the same directory where you originally issued the *checkout* command. This will be the parent directory of the module's top-level source directory. If you don't specify a *modulename*, CVS will update only the files in and below your current working directory.

Here is an example session in which a module is checked out, its contents perused, and its source updated to the latest version:

```
% cvs checkout testmodule
cvs checkout: Updating testmodule
U testmodule/Makefile
U testmodule/bar.c
U testmodule/foo.c
% cd testmodule/
% ls -l
total 24
drwxr-xr-x  5 bjepson  staff  126 Apr 10 13:23 CVS
-rw-r--r--  1 bjepson  staff    3 Apr 10 13:22 Makefile
-rw-r--r--  1 bjepson  staff    2 Apr 10 13:22 bar.c
-rw-r--r--  1 bjepson  staff    2 Apr 10 13:22 foo.c

*** time passes ***

% cvs update -P -d
cvs update: Updating .
U bar.c
% ls -l bar.c
-rw-r--r--  1 bjepson  staff  2 Apr 10 13:23 bar.c
```

Getting the Right Version

The only version of Darwin that should work with your copy of Mac OS X is the same one that Apple used. Your mileage may vary if you try to use an older or newer version. So, before you try anything like that, get the correct version and use that as a dry run to verify that you can build and install a working kernel.

First, find your Darwin version with the *uname -v* command. The output you're looking for is the *xnu* (Darwin kernel) version, shown in *italic* type:

```
% uname -v
Darwin Kernel Version 6.0: Sat Jul 27 13:18:52 PDT 2002;
root:xnu/xnu-344.obj~1/RELEASE_PPC
```

You need to translate that number into an Apple CVS tag, by replacing the period (.) with a dash (-) and prefixing the version with Apple-. So, the Apple CVS tag for the *xnu* version previously shown would be Apple-344. This is the version you must supply with the *-r* flag. Now that you know the CVS tag, you can check it out:

```
cvs -z3 checkout -r APPLE_CVS_TAG modulename
```

Where *APPLE_CVS_TAG* is the CVS tag you computed, and *modulename* is *xnu*. For example:

```
% cvs -z3 checkout -r Apple-344
cvs server: Updating xnu
U xnu/APPLE_LICENSE
U xnu/Makefile
U xnu/PB.project
U xnu/README
.
.
.
```

 The CVS tags are symbolic names associated with a snapshot of the source code in time. An easy way to browse the available tags is through the Darwin CVSWeb archive, available at *http://www.opensource.apple.com/tools/cvs/*. You will need to provide your registered username and password to access the archive. You can also use CVSWeb to peruse the archive and view the source code.

Building and Installing the Kernel

Now that you have downloaded the source from CVS, you can change to the *xnu* directory and load some environment variables. If you're using *tcsh*, you can use the following commands:

```
% cd xnu
% source SETUP/setup.csh
```

If you're using *bash* or *zsh*, you can use these commands:

```
$ cd xnu
$ . SETUP/setup.sh
```

To build the kernel, use this command (the output is not shown):

```
% make
```

When *make* is finished, you should see *mach_kernel* in the *xnu/BUILD/obj/ RELEASE_PPC* directory. Before you install the new kernel, back up your old kernel as follows:

```
% sudo cp /mach_kernel /mach_kernel.backup
```

Next, copy the new kernel over the older version:

```
% sudo cp BUILD/obj/RELEASE_PPC/mach_kernel /
```

Cross your fingers, knock on wood, and reboot. If all goes well, you should see the build time, hostname, and your username (since you're the person who compiled the kernel) when you run *uname -v*:

```
Darwin Kernel Version 6.0: Thu Aug 22 15:52:19 EDT 2002;
bjepson:BUILD/obj/RELEASE_PPC
```

Once you've made it that far, you can start modifying the code or experimenting with unofficial patches!

Kernel Configuration

Darwin includes configuration directories for each major component of the operating system, as listed here:

xnu/bsd/conf
> Contains configuration files for the BSD portions of Darwin.

xnu/iokit/conf
> Contains configuration files for IOKit, Darwin's subsystem for device drivers.

xnu/libkern/conf
> Contains configuration files for *libkern*, a set of base classes for kernel C++ code.

xnu/libsa/conf
> Contains configuration files for implementations of standard C library functions that are used by the kernel.

xnu/osfmk/conf
> Contains configuration files for the Mach portions of Darwin.

xnu/pexpert/conf
> Contains configuration files for pexpert (platform expert). This is for low-level hardware support during the boot sequence.

libsa and pexpert are private to the *xnu* kernel and should not be used by kernel extensions.

To tweak machine-independent aspects of a Darwin kernel component, you can edit the *MASTER* file in each configuration directory. You can find machine-dependent configuration options in *MASTER.i386* (for *x*86 systems) and *MASTER.ppc* (for PowerPC systems).

CHAPTER 8

System Management Tools

Mac OS X comes with many tools for tweaking and spying on various aspects of your system, including memory, kernel modules, and kernel state variables. Some of these tools come directly from BSD, while others are unique to Mac OS X. Most of the BSD-derived utilities have been filtered through Mach and NeXTSTEP on their way to Mac OS X.

For more details on any of these utilities, see their respective manpages.

Diagnostic Utilities

Mac OS X includes many diagnostic utilities that you can use to monitor your system and investigate problems.

top

The *top* utility displays memory statistics and a list of running processes. It is divided into two regions: the top region contains memory statistics and the bottom region contains details on each process.

 The Mac OS X version of *top* is based on the one used in early versions of BSD. It was ported to Mach in 1988, to NeXTSTEP in 1990, and to Mac OS X in 1999.

You can specify the number of processes to show by supplying a numeric argument. By default, *top* refreshes its display every second and sorts the list of processes by process ID (PID) in descending order. You can set *top* to sort by CPU utilization with *-u*, and you can specify the refresh delay with the *-s* option. Figure 8-1 shows the output of *top -u 10* (if you wanted to refresh the output every 3 seconds, you could run *top -s3 -u 10*).

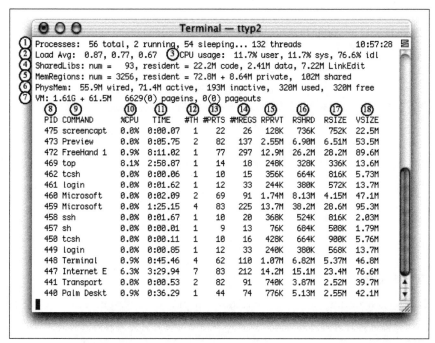

Figure 8-1. Sample output from top

Table 8-1 describes the values shown in the top region, and Table 8-2 describes the columns in the bottom region (process information).

Table 8-1. Memory information displayed by top

Item number	Item	Description
1	Processes	The number of processes and threads. A running process is currently using CPU time, while a sleeping process is not.
2	Load Avg.	The average system load (number of jobs vying for the CPU's attention) over the last 1, 5, and 15 minutes.
3	CPU usage	A breakdown of CPU usage, listing time spent in user mode, kernel (sys) mode, and idle time.
4	SharedLibs	The number of shared libraries in use, along with their memory utilization.
5	MemRegions	The number of Mach virtual memory regions in use, along with memory utilization details.
6	PhysMem	The physical memory utilization. Memory that is wired cannot be swapped to disk. active memory is memory that's currently being used, inactive memory is memory that Mac OS X is keeping "on deck" for processes that need it, and free memory is memory that's not being used at all.
7	VM	The virtual memory statistics, including the total amount of virtual memory allocated (the sum of the VSIZE in the process list), as well as paging activity (data paged in and out of physical memory).

Table 8-2. Process information displayed by top

Item number	Item	Description
8	PID	Process ID
9	COMMAND	Program's name
10	%CPU	Percentage of the CPU that the process is using
11	TIME	Total amount of CPU time this process has used
12	#TH	Number of threads in this process
13	#PRTS	Number of Mach ports
14	#MREGS	Number of memory registers
15	RPRVT	Resident private memory
16	RSHRD	Resident shared memory
17	RSIZE	Resident memory
18	VSIZE	Process's total address space, including shared memory

fs_usage

The *fs_usage* utility shows a continuous display of filesystem-related system calls and page faults. You must run *fs_usage* as *root*. By default, it ignores anything originating from *fs_usage*, *Terminal*, *telnetd*, *sshd*, *rlogind*, *tcsh*, *csh*, or *sh*.

Figure 8-2 shows the output of *fs_usage*, which displays the:

1. Timestamp
2. System call
3. Filename
4. Elapsed time
5. Name of the process

latency

latency measures the number of context switches and interrupts, and reports on the resulting delays, updating the display once per second. This utility must be run as *root*. Example 8-1 shows a portion of its output.

Example 8-1. Partial output from latency

```
Mon Apr  8 16:30:30                                    0:01:58
                        SCHEDULER       INTERRUPTS
-----------------------------------------------------
total_samples              64431           179982

delays <  10 usecs         38731           176120
```

Example 8-1. Partial output from latency (continued)

```
delays <  20 usecs    10763      2885
delays <  30 usecs     2934       447
delays <  40 usecs     1037       190
delays <  50 usecs      718        93
delays <  60 usecs      708        41
delays <  70 usecs      540        32
delays <  80 usecs      420        21
delays <  90 usecs      310        30
delays < 100 usecs      217        20
total  < 100 usecs    56378    179879
```

The SCHEDULER column lists the number of context switches and the
INTERRUPTS column lists the number of interrupts.

sc_usage

The *sc_usage* utility samples system calls and page faults, displaying them
onscreen. *sc_usage* must be run by *root* or by someone who has superuser
privileges. The display is updated once per second. You must specify a PID,
a command name, or a program to execute with the *-E* switch. For example, to monitor the Finder, use *sc_usage Finder*. Figure 8-2 shows the output
of running *sc_usage* on the Finder. Table 8-3 explains *sc_usage*'s output.

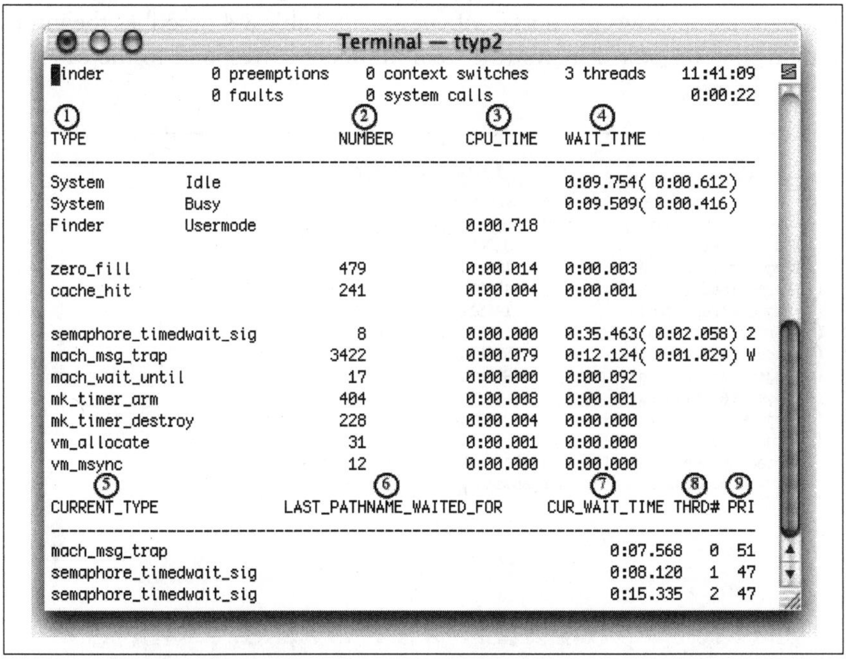

Figure 8-2. sc_usage monitoring the Finder

Table 8-3. Information displayed by sc_usage

Item number	Row	Description
1	TYPE	The system call type
2	NUMBER	The system call count
3	CPU_TIME	The processor time used by the system call
4	WAIT_TIME	The absolute time that the process spent waiting
5	CURRENT_TYPE	The current system call type
6	LAST_PATHNAME_WAITED_FOR	The last file or directory that resulted in a blocked I/O operation during a system call
7	CUR_WAIT_TIME	The cumulative time spent blocked
8	THRD#	The thread ID
9	PRI	The scheduling priority

vm_stat

The *vm_stat* utility displays virtual memory statistics. Unlike implementations of *vm_stat* in other Unix systems, it does not default to continuous display. Instead, it displays accumulated statistics.

To obtain a continuous display, specify an interval argument (in seconds), as in *vm_stat 1*. Figure 8-3 shows the output of *vm_stat* with no arguments, and Figure 8-4 shows the output of *vm_stat 1*. Table 8-4 describes the information that *vm_stat* displays (the item numbers correspond to the callouts in both figures).

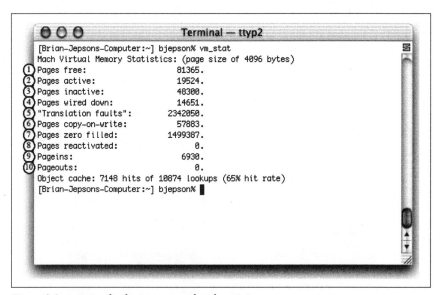

Figure 8-3. vm_stat displaying accumulated statistics

```
○ ○ ○                    Terminal — ttyp2
[Brian-Jepsons-Computer:~] bjepson% vm_stat 1
Mach Virtual Memory Statistics: (page size of 4096 bytes, cache hits 66%)
  free active inac wire  faults    copy zerofill reactive  pageins  pageout
78734 19729 50666 14711 2456422   58290 1596119        0     7006        0
78725 19729 50675 14711      14       0      11        0        0        0
78716 19729 50684 14711      14       0      11        0        0        0
78708 19729 50692 14711      13       0      10        0        0        0
78588 19782 50756 14714     409      88      56        0        1        0
78596 19782 50748 14714      27       5       8        0        0        0
78587 19782 50757 14714      14       0      11        0        0        0
78587 19782 50757 14714       5       0       2        0        0        0
78576 19782 50768 14714      17       0      13        0        0        0
78576 19782 50768 14714       5       0       2        0        0        0
78573 19782 50771 14714       9       0       5        0        0        0
78513 19782 50831 14714      67       0      63        0        0        0
78511 19782 50833 14714       7       0       4        0        0        0
78503 19782 50841 14714      13       0      10        0        0        0
78503 19782 50841 14714       6       0       2        0        0        0
78490 19782 50854 14714      18       0      15        0        0        0
78481 19782 50863 14714      14       0      11        0        0        0
78481 19782 50863 14714       5       0       2        0        0        0
78481 19782 50863 14714      22       0      19        0        0        0
78438 19782 50906 14714      48       0      45        0        0        0
78438 19782 50906 14714       5       0       2        0        0        0
 ① ② ③ ④   ⑤  ⑥  ⑦  ⑧  ⑨  ⑩
```

Figure 8-4. vm_stat's continuous output

Table 8-4. Information displayed by vm_stat

Item number	Accumulated mode	Continuous mode	Description
1	Pages free	free	Total free pages
2	Pages active	active	Total pages in use that can be paged out
3	Pages inactive	inac	Total inactive pages
4	Pages wired down	wire	Total pages wired into memory (cannot be paged out)
5	Translation Faults	faults	Number of times *vm_fault* has been called
6	Pages copy-on-write	copy	Number of faults that resulted in a page being copied
7	Pages zero filled	zerofill	Number of pages that have been zero-filled
8	Pages Reactivated	reactive	Number of pages reclassified from inactive to active
9	Pageins	pagein	Number of pages moved into physical memory
10	Pageouts	pageout	Number of pages moved out of physical memory

Kernel Utilities

Mac OS X includes various utilities that interact with the kernel. With these utilities, you can debug a running kernel, load and unload kernel modules or extensions, or set kernel variables.

ddb

The *ddb* utility can debug a running kernel. It is not included with the current version of Mac OS X. If you want to use *ddb*, you can find its source code in the *xnu* (Darwin kernel) source code. For details on building the kernel or obtaining source code from CVS, see Chapter 7.

Kernel Module Utilities

The following list describes utilities for manipulating kernel modules. For more information, see the kernel extension tutorials available at *http://www.opensource.apple.com/projects/documentation/howto*. These utilities must be run by *root* or by someone with superuser privileges.

kextload
  Loads an extension bundle.

kextunload
  Unloads an extension bundle.

kextstat
  Displays the status of currently loaded kernel extensions. Table 8-5 describes this utility's output.

Table 8-5. Information displayed by kextstat

Item number	Column	Description
1	Index	Index number of the loaded extension. Extensions are loaded in sequence; gaps in this sequence signify extensions that have been unloaded.
2	Refs	Number of references to this extension from other extensions.
3	Address	Kernel space address of the extension.
4	Size	Amount of kernel memory (in bytes) used by the extension.
5	Wired	Amount of *wired* kernel memory (in bytes) used by the extension.
6	Name (Version)	Name and version of the extension.
7	<Linked Against>	Index of kernel extensions to which this extension refers.

Figure 8-5 shows sample output.

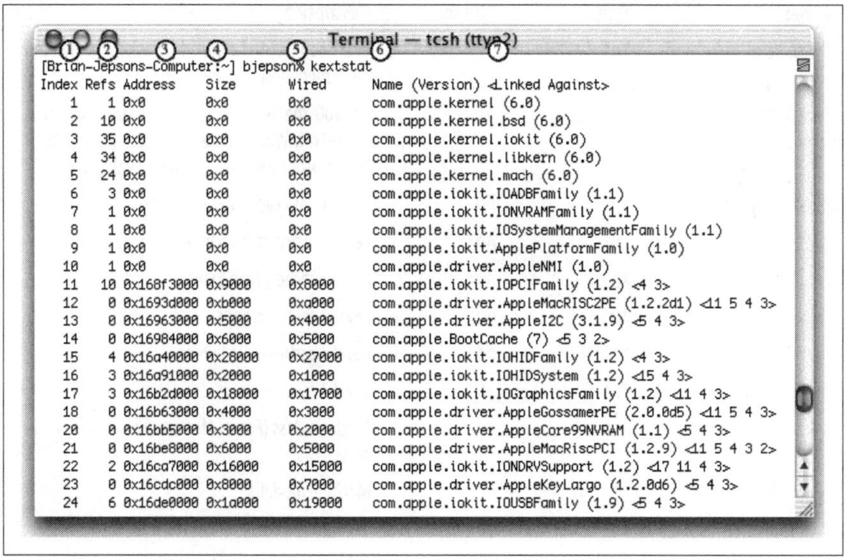

Figure 8-5. Partial output of kextstat

sysctl

sysctl is a standard BSD facility for configuring kernel state variables. Use *sysctl name* to display a variable name, as in *sysctl kern.ostype*. Use *sysctl -a* to display all variables. You can set a variable with *sysctl -w name=value*. You must have superuser privileges to set a variable.

Table 8-6 lists the *sysctl* variables on Mac OS X. See the *sysctl(3)* manpage for a description of the *sysctl* system call and more detailed information on the kernel state variables.

Table 8-6. sysctl's kernel state variables

Name	Type	Writable	Description
hw.busfrequency	int	no	Bus frequency in hertz. Divide by one million to get a megahertz figure.
hw.byteorder	int	no	Variable that returns 4321, showing the ordering of four bytes on the PowerPC platform.
hw.cachelinesize	int	no	The cache line size in bytes.

Table 8-6. sysctl's kernel state variables (continued)

Name	Type	Writable	Description
hw.cpufrequency	int	no	CPU frequency in hertz. Divide by one million to get a megahertz figure.
hw.epoch	int	no	Variable that indicates whether your hardware is in the New World or the Old World. Old World Macintoshes (pre-G3) will have a value of 0.
hw.l1dcachesize	int	no	Level 1 data cache size in bytes.
hw.l1icachesize	int	no	Level 1 instruction cache size in bytes.
hw.l2cachesize	int	no	Level 2 cache size in bytes.
hw.l2settings	int	no	Level 2 cache settings.
hw.l3cachesize	int	no	Level 3 cache size in bytes.
hw.l3settings	int	no	Level 3 cache settings.
hw.machine	string	no	Machine class (*Power Macintosh* on most systems).
hw.model	string	no	Machine model.
hw.ncpu	int	no	Number of CPUs.
hw.pagesize	int	no	Software page size in bytes.
hw.physmem	int	no	Physical memory in bytes.
hw.usermem	int	no	Non-kernel memory.
hw.vectorunit	int	no	Variable that indicates whether you are running on an AltiVec-enabled CPU.
kern.argmax	int	no	Maximum number of arguments supported by exec( ).
kern.boottime	struct timeval	no	The time when the system was booted.
kern.clockrate	struct clockinfo	no	System clock timings.
kern.dummy	n/a	n/a	Unused.
kern.hostid	int	yes	Host identifier.
kern.hostname	string	yes	Hostname.
kern.job_control	int	no	Variable that indicates whether job control is available.
kern.maxfiles	int	yes	Maximum number of open files.
kern.maxproc	int	yes	Maximum number of simultaneous processes.
kern.maxvnodes	int	yes	Maximum number of vnodes.
kern.ngroups	int	no	Maximum number of supplemental groups.
kern.netboot	int	no	Variable that indicates whether the system booted via NetBoot.
kern.nisdomainname	string	yes	NIS domain name.

Table 8-6. sysctl's kernel state variables (continued)

Name	Type	Writable	Description
kern.osrelease	string	no	Operating system release version.
kern.osrevision	int	no	Operating system revision.
kern.ostype	string	no	Operating system name.
kern.posix1version	int	no	The version of POSIX 1003.1 with which the system attempts to comply.
kern.saved_ids	int	no	This is set to 1 if saved set-group and set-user IDs are available.
kern.securelevel	int	increment only	The system security level.
kern.symfile	string	no	The kernel symbol file.
kern.sysv.shmmax	int	yes	The maximum number of shared memory pages.
kern.sysv.shmmin	int	yes	The maximum number of shared memory segments per process.
kern.sysv.shmmni	int	yes	The maximum number of shared memory segments.
kern.sysv.shmseg	int	yes	The minimum size of a shared memory segment.
kern.sysv.shmall	int	yes	The maximum size of a shared memory segment.
kern.version	string	no	The kernel version string.
net.inet.*	various	n/a	IPv4 settings.
net.key.*	various	n/a	IPSec key management settings.
net.inet6.*	various	n/a	IPv6 settings.
user.bc_base_max	int	no	Maximum ibase/obase available in the *bc* calculator.
user.bc_dim_max	int	no	Maximum array size available in the *bc* calculator.
user.bc_scale_max	int	no	Maximum scale value available in the *bc* calculator.
user.bc_string_max	int	no	Maximum string length available in the *bc* calculator.
user.coll_weights_max	int	no	Maximum number of weights that can be used with LC_COLLATE in the locale definition file.
user.cs_path	string	no	Value for PATH that can find all the standard utilities.
user.expr_nest_max	int	no	Maximum number of expressions you can nest within parentheses using *expr*.
user.line_max	int	no	Maximum length in bytes of an input line used with a text-processing utility.
user.posix2_c_bind	int	no	Variable that returns 1 if the C development environment supports the POSIX C Language Bindings Option; otherwise, the result will be 0.

Table 8-6. sysctl's kernel state variables (continued)

Name	Type	Writable	Description
user.posix2_c_dev	int	no	Variable that returns 1 if the C development environment supports the POSIX C Language Development Utilities Option; otherwise, the result will be 0.
user.posix2_char_term	int	no	Variable that returns 1 if the systems supports at least one terminal type specified in POSIX 1003.2; otherwise, the result will be 0.
user.posix2_fort_dev	int	no	Variable that returns 1 if the system supports the POSIX FORTRAN Development Utilities Option; otherwise, the result will be 0.
user.posix2_fort_run	int	no	Variable that returns 1 if the system supports the POSIX FORTRAN Runtime Utilities Option; otherwise, the result will be 0.
user.posix2_localedef	int	no	Variable that returns 1 if the system allows you to create locale; otherwise, the result will be 0.
user.posix2_sw_dev	int	no	Variable that returns 1 if the system supports the POSIX Software Development Utilities Option; otherwise, the result will be 0.
user.posix2_upe	int	no	Variable that returns 1 if the system supports the POSIX User Portable Utilities Option; otherwise, the result will be 0.
user.posix2_version	int	no	Variable that returns the POSIX 1003.2 version with which the system attempts to comply.
user.re_dup_max	int	no	Maximum repeated occurrences of a regular expression when using interval notation.
user.stream_max	int	no	Maximum number of streams a process may have open.
user.tzname_max	int	no	Maximum number of types supported for a time zone name.

System Configuration

Although you can perform most system configuration through the System Preferences program, the *defaults* command lets you poke around under the hood. You can get even further under the hood with the *nvram* command (perhaps further than most people would need or want to get).

defaults

When you customize your Mac using the System Preferences, all of those changes and settings are stored in what's known as the defaults system. Everything that you've done to make your Mac your own is stored as XML data in the form of a *property list* (or *plist*). This property list is, in turn, stored in *~/Library/Preferences*.

Every time you change one of those settings, that particular property list is updated. For the initiated, there are two other ways to alter the property lists. The first is by using the PropertyListEditor application (*/Developer/ Applications*) and the other is by using the *defaults* command in the Terminal. Whether you use System Preferences, PropertyListEditor, or the *defaults* command, any changes you make affect the current user.

Syntax

```
defaults [-currentHost | -host name] command
```

Options

-currentHost
> Performs operations on the local machine.

-host name
> Performs operations on the specified host.

Commands

read
> Prints out all of your current settings.

read domain
> Prints out your settings for the specified domain, such as *com.apple. dock*.

read domain key
> Prints out the value of the specified key. For example, to see the current Dock orientation, use:
> ```
> defaults read com.apple.dock orientation.
> ```

read-type domain key
> Prints out the data type of the specified key. For example, *defaults read-type com.apple.dock orientation* tells you that the type of the *orientation* key is *string*.

write domain key value
> Writes a value to the specified key.

rename domain old_key new_key
> Renames the specified key.

delete domain
> Deletes the specified domain. So, if you issued the command *defaults delete com.apple.dock*, the Dock would forget everything. The next time you log in, the Dock's settings are set to the system default.

delete domain key

Deletes the specified key. So, if you issued the command *defaults delete com.apple.dock orientation*, the Dock would forget its *orientation*. The next time you log in, the Dock's settings are set to the system default.

domains

Lists all the domains in your defaults.

find string

Searches all defaults for the specified string.

help

Prints a list of options.

Values

A value may take one of the following forms:

string

Specifies a string value. For example, *defaults write com.apple.dock orientation right*.

-type value

Specifies a value of the specified type. The type may be *string, float,* or *boolean*. For example, *defaults write com.apple.dock autohide -boolean true*.

-array [-add] value [value ...]

Creates or adds to a list of defaults. For example, you can create a list of your favorite colors with *defaults write personal.favorites colors -array red, blue*. Use *-add* to add values to an existing array.

-dict [-add] key value [key value...]

Creates or adds to a dictionary list. For example, you can create a dictionary of preferred pet foods with *defaults write personal.pets food -dict cat salmon dog steak*.

Using the *defaults* command is not for the foolhardy. If you manage to mangle your settings, the easiest way to correct the problem is to go back to that application's Preferences pane and reset your preferences. In some cases, you can use *defaults delete*, which will be reset to the same defaults when you next log in. Since the *defaults* command affects only the current user, you could also create a user just for testing random *defaults* tips you pick up on the Internet.

Examples

View all of the user defaults on your system

```
% defaults domains
```

This will print a listing of all of the *domains* in the user's defaults system. The list you'll see is run together with spaces in between—not quite the prettiest way to view the information.

View the settings for your Terminal

```
% defaults read com.apple.Terminal
```

This command reads the settings from the *com.apple.Terminal.plist* file, found in *~/Library/Preferences*. This listing is rather long, so you might want to pipe the output to *less* or *more* to view the contents one screen at a time:

```
% defaults read com.apple.Terminal | more
```

Change your Dock's default location to the top of the screen

```
% defaults write com.apple.Dock orientation top
```

This moves the Dock to the top of the screen underneath the menu bar. After changing that setting, you'll need to logout from the system and then log back in to see the Dock under the menu bar.

nvram

The *nvram* utility modifies Open Firmware variables, which control the boot-time behavior of your Macintosh. To list all Open Firmware variables, use *nvram -p*. The Apple Open Firmware page is *http://bananajr6000.apple.com/*.

To change a variable, you must run *nvram* as *root* or as the superuser. To set a variable, use *variable=value*. For example, to configure Mac OS X to boot verbosely, use *nvram boot-args=-v*. (Booting into Mac OS 9 or earlier will reset this.) Table 8-7 lists Open Firmware variables. Some variables use the Open Firmware Device Tree notation (see the technotes available at the Apple Open Firmware page).

 Be careful changing the *nvram* utility, since incorrect settings can turn a G4 iMac into a $2000 doorstop. If you render your computer unbootable, you can reset Open Firmware by zapping the PRAM. To zap the PRAM, hold down Option-⌘-P-R as you start the computer, and then release the keys when you hear a second startup chime. (If your two hands are busy holding down the other buttons and you have trouble reaching the power button, remember that you can press it with your nose.)

Table 8-7. nvram variables

Variable	Description
auto-boot?	The automatic boot settings. If `true` (the default), Open Firmware will automatically boot an operating system. If `false`, the process will stop at the Open Firmware prompt. Be careful using this with Old World (unsupported) machines and third-party graphics adapters, since the display and keyboard may not be initialized until the operating system starts (in which case, you will not have access to Open Firmware).
boot-args	The arguments that are passed to the boot loader.
boot-command	The command that starts the boot process. The default is *mac-boot*, an Open Firmware command that examines the boot-device for a Mac OS startup.
boot-device	The device to boot from. The syntax is *device*:[*partition*],*path*:*filename*, and a common default is hd:,\\:tbxi. In the path, \\ is an abbreviation for */System/Library/CoreServices*, and tbxi is the file type of the *BootX* boot loader. (Run */Developer/Tools/GetFileInfo* on *BootX* to see its type.)
boot-file	The name of the boot loader. (This is often blank, since boot-command and boot-device are usually all that are needed.)
boot-screen	The image to display on the boot screen.
boot-script	A variable that can contain an Open Firmware boot script.
console-screen	A variable that specifies the console output device, using an Open Firmware Device Tree name.
default-client-ip	An IP address for diskless booting.
default-gateway-ip	A gateway address for diskless booting.
default-mac-address?	Description not available at time of writing; see errata page at *http://www.oreilly.com/catalog/mosxgeeks*.
default-router-ip	A router address for diskless booting.
default-server-ip	An IP address for diskless booting.
default-subnet-mask	A default subnet mask for diskless booting.
diag-device	A private variable; not usable for security reasons.
diag-file	A private variable; not usable for security reasons.
diag-switch?	A private variable; not usable for security reasons.
fcode-debug?	A variable that determines whether the Open Firmware Forth interpreter will display extra debugging information.
input-device	The input device to use for the Open Firmware console.
input-device-1	A secondary input device (so you can have a screen and serial console at the same time). Use *scca* for the first serial port.
little-endian?	The CPU endian-ness. If `true`, initializes the PowerPC chip as little-endian. The default is `false`.
load-base	A private variable; not usable for security reasons.
mouse-device	The mouse device using an Open Firmware Device Tree name.
nvramrc	A sequence of commands to execute at boot time (if *use-nvramc?* is set to true).

Table 8-7. nvram variables (continued)

Variable	Description
oem-banner	A custom banner to display at boot time.
oem-banner?	The oem banner settings. Set to `true` to enable the oem banner. The default is `false`.
oem-logo	A 64-by-64 bit array containing a custom black-and-white logo to display at boot time. This should be specified in hex.
oem-logo?	The oem logo settings. Set to `true` to enable the oem logo. The default is `false`.
output-device	The device to use as the system console. The default is `screen`.
output-device-1	A secondary output device (so you can have everything go to both the screen and a serial console). Use *scca* for the first serial port.
pci-probe-mask	A private variable; not usable for security reasons.
ram-size	The amount of RAM currently installed. For example, 256 MB is shown as 0x10000000.
real-base	The starting physical address that is available to Open Firmware.
real-mode?	The address translation settings. If `true`, Open Firmware will use real-mode address translation. Otherwise, it uses virtual-mode address translation.
real-size	The size of the physical address space available to Open Firmware.
screen-#columns	The number of columns for the system console.
screen-#rows	The number of rows for the system console.
scroll-lock	Set by page checking output words to prevent Open Firmware text from scrolling off the top of the screen.
selftest-#megs	The number of MB of RAM to test at boot time. The default is 0.
use-generic?	The device node naming settings. Specifies whether to use generic device node names such as 'screen', as opposed to Apple hardware code names.
use-nvramrc?	The command settings. If this is `true`, Open Firmware uses the commands in *nvramrc* at boot time.
virt-base	The starting virtual address that is available to Open Firmware.
virt-size	The size of the virtual address space available to Open Firmware.

## CHAPTER 9

The X Window System

Although the X in "Mac OS X" is not the same X as in "The X Window System," you can get them to play nice together.

Most Unix systems use the X Window System as their GUI. (We'll refer to the X Window System as X11, to avoid confusion with Mac OS X.) X11 includes development tools and libraries for creating graphical applications for Unix-based systems. Mac OS X does not use X11 as its GUI, relying instead on Quartz (and, on compatible hardware, Quartz Extreme), a completely different graphics system. However, an implementation of X11 for Mac OS X is available from the XFree86 Project (*http://www.xfree86.org/*). The XDarwin project (*http://www.xdarwin.org/*) provides an easy-to-install binary distribution of XFree86.

Installing X11

The XFree86 site contains instructions for downloading and installing the X11R6 binaries on a Mac OS X system. The site also provides instructions for compiling the X11R6 suite from source. The easiest way to get X11 for Mac OS X is through either XDarwin or Fink, both of which contain easy-to-install binary distributions of X11. Fink also includes the *system-xfree86* package, which is a placeholder package that lets you use the X11 distribution of your choice with Fink. (The placeholder package satisfies the same dependencies as the Fink X11 package.)

Manually Installing X11

If you want to install the XFree86 distribution manually, download the distribution (see the instructions on the XFree86 web site) and run the *Xinstall.sh* script to install the XFree86 suite.

This script will prompt you for some configuration details, although it includes defaults that should work for most Mac OS X users. The XFree86 web site has an extensive set of instructions explaining how to install XFree86 for the first time, how to install the suite over an older XFree86 installation, and how to uninstall XFree86. There are specific instructions for Mac OS X and Darwin.

The installer script will install the X11 binaries, libraries, header files, manpages, configuration files, etc., in */usr/X11R6* and */etc/X11*.

There is very little difference between manually installing XFree86 on Mac OS X and manually installing it on other Unix systems. The main difference is that some files required on other Unix systems are not required on Darwin. For example, there is no separate *Xvar.tgz* file to download. Another difference with Mac OS X is that the double-clickable XDarwin application is placed in the */Applications* folder.

Running XDarwin

XDarwin can be run in two modes: *full screen* or *rootless*. Either of these modes runs side-by-side with Aqua, although full-screen mode hides the Finder desktop. To launch the X server, double-click the XDarwin application (*/Applications*). You will be prompted to choose which of these two modes to run. In rootless mode, X11 applications take up their own window on your Aqua desktop. In full-screen mode, X11 takes over the entire screen and is suitable if you want to run an X11 desktop environment (DTE) like GNOME, KDE, or Xfce. If you prefer rootless mode, you will probably want to run OroborOSX, an X window manager with a look and feel similar to Aqua (see the section "Aqua-like X Windows: OroborOSX," later in this chapter).

 You can still access your Mac OS X desktop while in full-screen mode by pressing Option-⌘-A. To go back to the X11 desktop, either press Option-⌘-A or click the XDarwin icon in the Dock.

Running XDarwin from the Console

You can also run XDarwin from the Darwin console. To run X11 from the Darwin console, first shut down Core Graphics by logging into the machine as >*console*. When the console prompt appears, log in with your normal username. Once logged in, start the X server by entering the command *exec startx*. To quit X11, type *exit* from the main login Terminal window. If there is a long delay, with only the spinning beach ball cursor visible, type *logout* to return to console mode. Note that in this situation, you will not see text appear on the screen as you type.

Desktops and Window Managers

You can do a lot of X11 customization in XDarwin. The most significant customization is in your choice of Window manager. To start customizing, you would typically use the *.xinitrc* script in the your home directory. A sample *.xinitrc* script is provided in */etc/X11/xinit/xinitrc*.

Using the script as a starting point, you can specify which X11-based applications to start when XDarwin is launched, including which window manager you'd like to use as your default. The default window manager for XDarwin is the tab window manager (or *twm*), but many other DTEs are available. You can visit the following web sites to get instructions and binaries for a wide variety of window managers and DTEs.

Fink
   http://fink.sourceforge.net

GNU-Darwin
   http://gnu-darwin.sourceforge.net

OroborOSX
   http://oroborosx.sourceforge.net

Once you've installed XFree86, you will probably want to install additional X11 applications, window managers, and perhaps other DTEs. One of the easiest ways to install additional window managers is to use Fink. Table 9-1 lists some of the window managers and desktops that can be installed via Fink. (For information on installing and updating Fink, see the "Fink" section in Chapter 6.)

Table 9-1. Window managers available for Fink

Window manager/desktop	Fink package name
Blackbox	*blackbox*
Enlightenment	*enlightenment*
FVWM	*fvwm, fvwm2*
GNOME	*bundle-gnome*
IceWM	*icewm*
KDE	As of this writing, support for KDE is available, but is experimental. See *http://fink.sourceforge.net/news/kde.php*.
mwm	*lesstif*

Table 9-1. Window managers available for Fink (continued)

Window manager/desktop	Fink package name
Oroborus	*oroborus, oroborus2*
PWM	*pwm*
Sawfish	*sawfish*
Window Maker	*windowmaker*
XFce	*xfce*

Fink has an entire section devoted to GNOME, where you will find an extensive set of GNOME libraries, utilities, and plug-ins. Also included in the GNOME section are GTK+, *glib*, and Glade. You can use Fink to install an *xterm* replacement such as *rxvt* or *eterm*.

It is important to remember that Fink installs everything in its */sw* directory. So, for example, if you've installed *lesstif* and want to use the *mwm* window manager, you must include your path in */sw/bin*, or include */sw/bin/mwm &* in your *.xinitrc* file to start the Motif window manager.

X11-based Applications and Libraries

You can also use Fink to install many X11-based applications, such as the GNU Image Manipulation Program (GIMP), *xfig/transfig*, ImageMagick, *nedit*, and many others. Since Fink understands dependencies, installing some of these applications will cause Fink to first install several other packages. For example, since the text editor *nedit* depends on Motif libraries, Fink will first install *lesstif*. (This also gives you the Motif window manager, *mwm*.) Similarly, when you install the GIMP via Fink, you will also install the packages for GNOME, GTK+, and *glib*.

You can also use Fink to install libraries directly. For example:

```
% fink install qt
```

will install the X11-based Qt libraries. An Aqua version of Qt for Mac OS X is available from Trolltech (*http://www.trolltech.com*).

Building X11-based Applications and Libraries

If you cannot find binaries for X11-based applications (or if you prefer to build the applications yourself), most of the tools to do this are available. First, you need Apple's Developer Tools. If you installed XFree86 by hand, make sure you installed *XProg.tgz*, which contains development tools and header files needed for building X11-based applications. The XDarwin distribution includes these tools and header files.

The process of building software usually begins with generating one or more *makefiles* customized to your system. For X11 applications, there are two popular methods for generating makefiles. One method is to use a *configure* script (see the "Compiling Unix Source Code" section in Chapter 4.)

The other popular method for generating makefiles involves using the *xmkmf* script, which is a frontend to the *imake* utility. *xmkmf* invokes *imake*, which creates a makefile. To do this, *imake* looks for a template file called *Imakefile*.

With *imake*-driven source releases, after downloading a source tarball, unpacking it, and changing to the top-level source directory, you'll find an *Imakefile*. After reading the *README* or *INSTALL* files, examine the *Imakefile* to see if you need to change anything. Then the next step is usually to issue the command:

```
% xmkmf -a
```

When invoked with the *-a* option, *xmkmf* reads *imake*-related files in */usr/X11R6/lib/X11/config* and performs the following tasks recursively, beginning in the top-level directory and then in the subdirectories, if there are any:

```
% make Makefiles
% make includes
% make depend
```

The next steps are usually *make*, *make test* (or *make check*), and *make install*.

To illustrate this method of building software, consider the script in Example 9-1, which downloads and builds an X11-based game.

Example 9-1. Downloading and building an X11 game

```
# Download the source tarball
curl -O ftp://ftp.x.org/contrib/games/xtic1.12.tar.gz

# Unpack the tarball
gnutar xvfz xtic1.12.tar.gz

# Change to the top-level build directory
cd xtic1.12/

# Generate the Makefile
xmkmf -a

# Build everything (some X11 apps use 'make World')
make

# Have fun!
./src/xtic
```

Making X11 Applications More Aqua-like

Even though you can run the X server in rootless mode and display X11 applications alongside Aqua applications, the appearance of X11 windows is determined by the window manager you are using. OroborOSX is a Window manager with a look and feel similar to Aqua, and AquaTerm displays vector graphics in an Aqua window.

An Aqua-like X11: OroborOSX

OroborOSX, developed by Adrian Umpleby, is a modified version of the *oroborus* GNOME-compliant X11 window manager created by Ken Lynch. OroborOSX is designed to make X windows look and behave as much like Aqua as possible.

Although OroborOSX includes a copy of the XDarwin server, it does not include supporting files such as user binaries, headers, and libraries. So, you should install XFree86 before running OroborOSX. Aside from the prerequisite software, one of the most Mac-like features of OroborOSX is its installation.

After unpacking the tarball containing the OroborOSX package, drag the OroborOSX folder to the Applications folder in the Finder. You might also consider adding its icon to the Dock.

Some versions of StuffIt Expander and the OroborOSX package do not play nice together. For best results, you should download the OroborOSX tarball, save it in the */Applications* directory, and unpack it there from the command line. For more details about this problem, see the OroborOSX FAQ page at *http://oroborosx.sourceforge.net*.

At the time of this writing, the latest version of OroborOSX is v0.8b2—a pre-Jaguar beta. To prevent XDarwin from crashing, you need to download an update for the *xterm* from the following web site: *http://prdownloads.sourceforge. net/xonx/Jaguar_XTerm_Update.zip?download*.

To launch OroborOSX, double-click its icon. Launching OroborOSX also starts XDarwin in the background.

You will notice some differences immediately. The first and most obvious difference from other X11 window managers is that the *xterm* window frames look very similar to the Aqua Terminal windows. In particular, they have the Aqua-like buttons for closing, minimizing, and maximizing the window. Also, OroborOSX windows minimize to the Dock, just like other Aqua windows. (Other X11 window managers have their own locations for minimized windows). Figure 9-1 shows a Terminal window and an xterm window side-by-side.

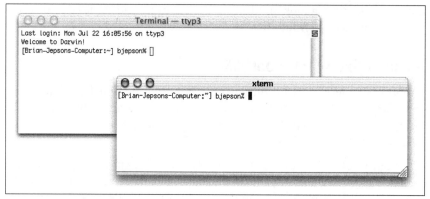

Figure 9-1. A Terminal and an xterm sporting the Aqua look

OroborOSX also includes the following features that distinguish it from other X11 window managers.

- X11 windows are interleaved with Aqua windows. Clicking an open OroborOSX window brings only that individual window to the front of the desktop, not all X11 windows.

- Clicking in a background window will bring that window to the front, but it won't pass the click through to any window controls. For example, if you click on the GIMP toolbar while it is in the background, this will only bring it to the front. Click again to select the tool you wanted.

- A list of X11 windows can be obtained by Control-clicking OroborOSX's icon in the Dock (and via the Window menu).

- New X11 application icons can be created with the *template* script. This file is located in the *Contents/Resources/Launch Menu Items* subdirectory of the OroborOSX application (*.app*) folder. Copy it to a file with an *.x11app* extension, edit it to suit your needs, and double-click it from the Finder to launch it under OroborOSX.

- X11 applications, such as *nedit* and the GIMP, can be launched from the Launch menu. You can also use the Launch menu to edit startup and launch items.

- X11 applications can be launched by double-clicking on their icons.

OroborOSX is a self-contained package. It does not interfere with any Unix-based software, although it can run X11 binaries that were installed by other packages.

By default, OroborOSX does not execute your *.xinitrc* script; however, this script can be run from OroborOSX's Launch menu. If you want to utilize your *.xinitrc* script this way, be sure not to start some other window manager in it. To prevent that from happening, simply comment out the line in your *.xinitrc* file that starts a window manager. For example, the following line:

```
exec mwm
```

should be changed to:

```
# exec mwm
```

One interesting Mac-like feature of OroborOSX is that double-clicking the titlebar of an OroborOSX window will window-shade it. This feature gives OroborOSX something in common with Mac OS 9 that Mac OS X windows lack; double-clicking a Mac OS X window's titlebar will minimize the window and place it in the Dock. The Window menu includes shortcuts for activating the window-shade feature, minimizing a window, or zooming a window. Figure 9-2 shows a window-shaded and normal *xterm* next to each other.

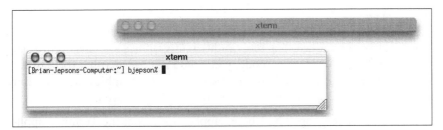

Figure 9-2. xterms with and without window shading

You can customize window appearance by choosing a different OroborOSX theme (Options → Themes). Here is a list of the OroborOSX themes:

Eau (default)
    This is an Aqua-like theme that styles the window and its titlebar to look just like normal Aqua windows under Mac OS X.

Greyphite
    This theme gives the windows an Aqua-like look and feel, but with a graphite style.

Nextish
    This theme creates windows with a NeXTSTEP appearance.

AquaTerm

The X Window System is useful to Unix developers and users, since many Unix-based software packages depend on the X11 libraries. An interesting project that in some cases eliminates the need for the X windows is the BSD-licensed AquaTerm application, developed by Per Persson (*http://aquaterm. sourceforge.net*). AquaTerm is a Cocoa application that can display vector graphics in an X11-like fashion. It does not replace X11, but it is useful for applications that need to generate plots and graphs.

The output graphics formats that AquaTerm supports are PDF and EPS. Applications communicate with AquaTerm through an adapter that acts as an intermediary between your old application's API and AquaTerm's API.

At the time of this writing, AquaTerm has are adapters for *gnuplot* and *PGPLOT*, as well as example adapters in C, FORTRAN, and Objective-C. For example, assuming that you have installed both XFree86 and Aqua-Term, you can build *gnuplot* (*http://www.gnuplot.info*) so that graphics can be displayed either in X windows or in AquaTerm windows.

There is extensive documentation on AquaTerm's web site (listed earlier in this section). Consult that site for the latest developments, examples, and other documentation.

Aqua-X11 Interactions

Since X11-based applications rely on different graphics systems even when running XDarwin in rootless mode, you would not necessarily expect to see GUI interactions run smoothly between these two graphics systems. But actually, there are several such interactions that run very well.

First, it is possible to open X11-based applications from the Terminal application. To launch an X11-based application from the Terminal application, you need to set the shell environment variable DISPLAY as follows for *tcsh*:

```
setenv DISPLAY 0:0
```

If you are using a Bourne-compatible shell, such as *bash*, you could use the following:

```
DISPLAY="0:0"; export DISPLAY
```

 You may want to add this functionality to your startup configuration script *.tcshrc* (for *tcsh*) or *.bashrc* (for *bash*).

You can also copy and paste between X11 and Mac OS X applications. For example, to copy from an *xterm*, select some text with your mouse. This action places the selected text into the Mac clipboard. To paste the contents of the clipboard into a Mac OS X application (such as the Terminal), simply press ⌘-V to paste the text.

To copy from a Mac OS X application, highlight some text and press ⌘-C. The copied text can be pasted into an *xterm* window by pressing the middle button of a three-button mouse or by Command-clicking in the X11 application.

 In Aqua, Mac OS X emulates right-mouse clicks with Control-click. In XDarwin, you can configure key combinations that simulate two- and three-button mice. By default, Option-click simulates the middle mouse button, and ⌘-click simulates the right mouse button. To configure this in XDarwin, choose Preferences from the XDarwin menu. In OroborOSX, choose XDarwin Preferences from the Options menu.

Connecting to Other X Window Systems

You can connect from Mac OS X to other X window systems using *ssh* with X11 forwarding. If you use OpenSSH (which is included with Mac OS X), you must use the -X option to request X11 forwarding (the -2 option specifies the *ssh* version 2 protocol, as opposed to the older version 1 protocol). For example:

```
ssh -2 -X remotemachine -l username
```

As long as XDarwin is running, this can be entered in either an *xterm* window or in the Mac OS X Terminal. To have the X11 forwarding enabled in Terminal, you must have the DISPLAY variable set prior to making the connection, as noted earlier. (This will always be the case if the DISPLAY variable is set in your *.tcshrc* script.) It is also possible to create a double-clickable application that connects to a remote machine via *ssh2*, with X11 forwarding enabled. For example, you can use the following script for this purpose:

```
#!/bin/sh
ssh -2 -X remotemachine -l username
```

If you've installed the commercial version of *ssh* from *http://www.ssh.com*, the equivalent of the preceding script is as follows:

```
#!/bin/sh
ssh2 remotemachine -l username
```

The X11 forwarding flag is +x with the commercial *ssh*, but it is enabled by default, so that you need not include it in the command.

Using OroborOSX, you can add a Launch menu item to accomplish the same task. To do this, start by copying the template file found in the directory *~/Library/Preferences/OroborOSX/Launch Menu Items* to whatever you'd like to call this application. For example, suppose we want to connect to a remote machine named *chops* with a username of *sam*. We'll name the application Connect2Chops. Start by copying the template to *Connect2Chops.x11app*:

```
% cp template Connect2Chops.x11app
```

Next, edit the *Connect2Chops.x11app* file. You only need to change a couple of lines, since you'll be using an *xterm*. In particular:

```
# ARGUMENTS FOR THE COMMAND GO HERE (can be left blank)
set argums="-geometry 80x25 -ls -sb -sl 5000 -e ssh -2 -X chops -l sam"

# OPTIONAL TITLE STRING GOES HERE (uncomment this if wanted)
# note that an ID number, sent from OroborOSX, will be added in
# brackets after this string [eg, below would give "xterm (3)"]
set titlenam="Connect2Chops"
```

Save this file in *~/Library/Preferences/OroborOSX/Launch Menu Items*, then select Launch → Rebuild Launch Menu.

That's it! Now you'll be ready to launch the connection to the remote machine via the menu bar. Once you've connected to a machine running X Windows, you can start X11-based applications on the remote machine and display them on your Mac OS X machine. Figure 9-3 shows MATLAB running on a remote Sun workstation, but displayed on the local Mac OS X machine.

Virtual Network Computers

One of the attractive features of Mac OS X is the ease with which you can integrate a Mac OS X system into a Unix environment consisting of multiple Unix workstations that typically rely on X11 for their GUI. In the previous section, for example, we explained how to log in to a remote Unix machine, launch an X11 application, and display the application on your Mac. The reverse process is also possible. You can log into a remote Mac OS X machine from another computer, launch an application on the remote Mac OS X machine, and have the application display on your local machine. The local machine, meanwhile, can be running the X Window System,

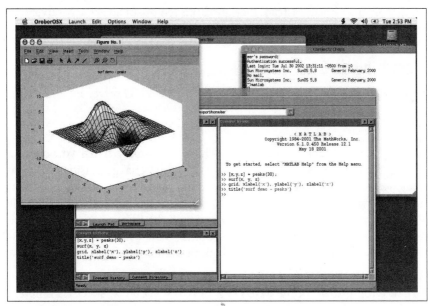

Figure 9-3. MATLAB running in a remote window on top of Mac OS X

Microsoft Windows, or any another platform supported by Virtual Network Computer (VNC).

VNC consists of two components: a VNC server (which must be installed on the remote machine) and a VNC viewer (which is used on the local machine to view and control applications running on the remote machine). The VNC connection is made through a TCP/IP connection.

The VNC server and viewer may not only be on different machines, but they can also be installed on different operating systems. This allows you to, for example, connect from Solaris to Mac OS X. Using VNC, you can launch and run X11 applications on Mac OS X, but view and control them from your Solaris box.

VNC can be installed on Mac OS X with the Fink package manager (look for the *vnc* package), but that version (the standard Unix version of the VNC server) only supports X11 programs, not Aqua applications. VNC translates X11 calls into the VNC protocol. All you need on the client machine is a VNC viewer.

The standard Unix version of the VNC server is quite robust. Rather than interacting with your display, it intercepts and translates the X11 network protocol. (In fact, the Unix version of the server is based on the XFree86 source code.) Applications that run under the Unix server are never displayed on the server's screen. Instead, they are displayed on an invisible X server that relays its virtual display to the VNC viewer on the client machine.

Launching VNC

If you installed VNC via Fink, you can start the VNC server by issuing the following command:

```
vncserver
```

You will need to enter a password, which you supply when you connect from a remote machine. (This password can be changed using the command *vncpasswd*.) You can run several servers; each server is identified by its hostname with a *:number* appended. For example, suppose you start the VNC server twice on a machine named *abbott*; the first server will be identified as *abbott:1* and the second as *abbott:2*. You will need to supply this identifier when you connect from a client machine.

By default, the VNC server runs *twm*. So, when you connect, you will see an X11 desktop instead of the Mac OS X desktop. (You can specify a different window manager in *~/.vnc/xstartup*.) To terminate the VNC server, use the following command syntax:

```
vncserver -kill :display
```

For example, to terminate *abbott:1*, you would issue the following command while logged into *abott* as the user who started the VNC server:

```
vncserver -kill :1.
```

 There is a derivative of VNC, called TightVNC, which is optimized for bandwidth conservations. It can also be installed with Fink. TightVNC also offers automatic *ssh* tunneling on Unix and backward compatibility with the standard VNC.

Connecting to the Mac OS X VNC Server

To connect to a Mac OS X machine that is running a VNC server, you will need a VNC viewer. Viewers are available for Mac OS X; a list can be found on Version Tracker (*http://www.versiontracker.com/macosx/*) by searching for "VNC".

If you want to connect to a VNC server from your Macintosh, there are several VNC viewers available for Mac OS X, including:

VNCDimension
   http://www.mdimension.com/Community/

VNCThing
   http://webthing.net/vncthing/

VNCViewer
   http://homepage.mac.com/kedoin/VNC/VNCViewer/

To connect, start your viewer and specify the hostname and display number, such as *abbott:1* or *abbott:2*. If all goes well, you'll be asked for your password, and then connected to the remote Mac OS X desktop.

Conclusion

From Aqua to X11, there's no shortage of graphical environments for Mac OS X. The operating system's solid Unix underpinnings and powerful graphics subsystem make it possible for developers to support alternative graphical environments. For this reason, a humble iBook can make the best cockpit for a network of heterogeneous machines!

Appendixes

There are two appendixes in this book:

- Appendix A, *The Mac OS X Filesystem*
- Appendix B, *Command-Line Tools: The Missing Manpages*

PART IV
Appendixes

The Mac OS X Filesystem

If you do an *ls -a /* on your Mac OS X box, you will see some familiar things, such as */etc* and */var*, but you will also notice some unfamiliar things, such as */TheVolumeSettingsFolder*, */Library*, and */Documents*. The Mac OS X filesystem contains traces of Unix, NeXTSTEP, and the Mac OS 9. This chapter describes the contents of important directories. The tables in this chapter list directory entries (directories are denoted with a trailing slash) and provide a description of each file or directory.

Files and Directories

Table A-1 describes the files and directories you may find in your *root* directory. The remaining tables in this chapter describe significant subdirectories.

Table A-1. Mac OS X's root directory

File or directory	Description
.DS_Store	This file contains Finder settings, such as icon location and window size. The file will appear in any directory that you've viewed with the Finder.
.Trashes/	This directory contains files that have been dragged to the Trash. On a boot volume, such files are stored in ~/.Trash. On a non-boot volume, these files are in /.Trashes/ uid/.
.hidden	This file contains a list of files that should be invisible to the Finder.
.vol/	This directory maps HFS+ file IDs to files. If you know a file's ID, you can open it using /.vol/id.
Applications (Mac OS 9)/	This directory contains all your OS 9 applications, if you've got Mac OS X and Mac OS 9 installed.
Applications/	This directory holds all your Mac OS X applications. Its *Utilities* subdirectory includes lots of useful things, such as Terminal and Console.
Desktop DB	This file, along with *Desktop DF*, contains the desktop database that is rebuilt when you click Rebuild Desktop in System Preferences → Classic.

File or directory	Description
Desktop DF	See *Desktop DB*.
Desktop Folder/	This directory is the Mac OS 9 desktop folder.
Developer/	This directory contains Apple's Developer Tools and documentation. This is only available if you have installed the Developer Tools.
Documents/	This is the Mac OS 9 documents folder.
Library/	This directory contains support files for locally installed applications, among other things. See Table A-4, later in this chapter.
Network/	This directory contains network-mounted *Application*, *Library*, and *Users* directories, as well as a *Servers* directory, which contains directories mounted by the *automount* daemon.
Shared Items/	In Mac OS 9, this folder gave multiuser systems a place where users could store files that other users could access.
System Folder/	This is the Mac OS 9 System Folder.
System/	This directory contains a subdirectory, *Library*, which holds support files for the system and system applications, among other things. See Table A-3, later in this chapter.
Temporary Items/	This directory contains temporary files used by Mac OS 9.
TheVolumeSettingsFolder/	This directory keeps track of details such as open windows and desktop printers.
Trash/	This directory is where Mac OS 9 stores deleted files until the Trash is emptied.
Users/	This directory contains home directories for the users on the system. The *root* user's home directory is */var/root*.
VM Storage	This is the Mac OS 9 virtual memory file.
Volumes/	This directory contains all mounted filesystems, including removable media and mounted disk images.
automount/	This directory handles static NFS mounts for the *automount* daemon.
bin/	This directory contains essential system binaries.
cores/	This directory is a symbolic link (or *symlink*) to */private/cores*. If core dumps are enabled (with *tcsh*'s *limit* and *bash/sh*'s *ulimit* commands—see the *tcsh* and *bash* manpages for more details), they will be created in this directory as *core.pid*.
dev/	This directory contains files that represent various devices. See Table A-6, later in this chapter.
etc/	This directory contains system configuration files. See Table A-2, later in this chapter. The directory is a symbolic link to */private/etc*.
lost+found	This directory stores orphaned files discovered by *fsck*.
mach	This is a symbolic link to the */mach.sym* file.
mach.sym	This file contains kernel symbols. It is generated during each boot by */etc/rc*.
mach_kernel	This is the Darwin kernel. See Chapter 7 for more information about the kernel.
private/	This private directory contains the *tmp*, *var*, *etc*, and *cores* directories.
sbin/	This directory contains executables for system administration and configuration.

File or directory	Description
tmp/	This directory holds temporary files. It is a symbolic link to */private/tmp*.
usr/	This directory contains BSD Unix applications and support files.
var/	This directory contains frequently modified files, such as log files. It is a symbolic link to */private/var*.

The /etc Directory

The */etc* directory contains configuration files for Unix applications and services, as well as scripts that control system startup. Table A-2 lists the contents of the */etc* directory.

Table A-2. The /etc directory

File or directory	Description
6to4.conf	Configuration file for encapsulating IPv6 within IPv4. See *ip6config(8)*.
X11/	X11 configuration directory. This will be present only if you have installed XDarwin.
acgid/	File that contains configuration files for *acgid*, a bridge between Apache and ACGI-capable scripting languages, such as AppleScript. Mac OS X Server only. For equivalent functionality under Mac OS X, see *http://www.sentman.com/acgi/*.
afpovertcp.cfg	File that causes Mac OS X to use TCP/IP as the default transport for Apple File Protocol (AFP). Use this file to configure the defaults for AFP over TCP/IP.
appletalk.cfg	AppleTalk configuration file for routing or multihoming. See the *appletalk.cfg(5)* manpage.
authorization	File that controls how applications, such as installers, can temporarily obtain *root* privileges.
bashrc	Global configuration file for *bash*, the Bourne-again shell.
crontab	*root*'s *crontab*. See "Default cron Jobs" in Chapter 2.
csh.cshrc	Global *csh* configuration file, processed when the shell starts up. If you have a *.cshrc* or *.tcshrc* file in your home directory, *tcsh* will execute its contents as well.
csh.login	Global *csh* login file, processed when a login shell starts up. If you have a *.login* file in your home directory, *tcsh* will execute its contents as well.
csh.logout	Global *csh* logout file, processed when a user logs out of a login shell.
cups/	Directory that contains configuration files for Common Unix Printing System (CUPS).
daily	*cron* job that is run once a day (see *crontab*). This is a symlink to */etc/periodic/daily/500.daily*.
defaults/	Directory that contains default configuration files for applications and utilities.
diskspacemonitor/	Configuration files for *diskspacemonitor*, which monitors the amount of free disk space. Mac OS X Server only.
dumpdates	Dump date records created by *dump(5)*, which is run by */etc/daily*.
find.codes	Description not available at time of writing; see errata page at *http://www.oreilly.com/catalog/mosxgeeks*.

Table A-2. The /etc directory (continued)

File or directory	Description
ftpusers	List of users who are prohibited from using FTP.
gdb.conf	Global *gdb* configuration file.
gettytab	Terminal configuration database.
group	Group permissions file. See Chapter 3 for more information.
hostconfig	System configuration file that controls many of the startup items described in the "SystemStarter" section in Chapter 2.
hosts	Host database; a mapping of IP addresses to hostnames. You can use this as a supplement to other Directory Services, such as DNS. Mac OS X 10.1 and earlier consulted this file only in single-user mode, but Mac OS X 10.2 (Jaguar) uses this file at other times. For more information, see Chapter 3.
hosts.equiv	List of trusted remote hosts and host-user pairs. This is used by *rsh* and is inherently insecure. You should use *ssh* instead, which is a secure alternative. See *ssh-keygen(1)* to generate key pairs that can be used to set up a trust relationship with remote users.
hosts.lpd	List of hosts that are allowed to connect to the Unix *lpd* service.
httpd/	Directory that contains Apache's configuration files.
iftab	Configuration file for network interfaces.
inetd.conf	Internet super-server (*inetd*) configuration file.
IPAliases	Configuration file for IP aliases.
kcpassword	Description not available at time of writing; see errata page at *http://www.oreilly.com/catalog/mosxgeeks*.
kern_loader.conf	Description not available at time of writing; see errata page at *http://www.oreilly.com/catalog/mosxgeeks*.
localtime	Symbolic link to your system's time zone, such as: */usr/share/zoneinfo/US/Eastern*.
magic	Database of magic numbers used by the *file* command to determine a file's type.
mail/	Directory that contains configuration files for *sendmail*. Note that Open Directory handles the mail aliases (see Chapter 3).
mail.rc	Global configuration file for */usr/bin/mail*.
manpath.config	Configuration file for *man*.
master.passwd	Shadow *passwd* file. This is consulted only in single-user mode. During normal system operation, Open Directory manages user information (see Chapter 3).
moduli	System-wide prime numbers used for cryptographic applications such as *ssh*.
monthly	Monthly *cron* job (see *crontab*). This is a symlink to */etc/periodic/monthly/500.monthly*.
motd	Message of the day. This is displayed each time you launch a new Terminal or log in remotely.
named.conf	Configuration file for *named*, the DNS daemon. For more details, see *named(8)*.
networks	Network name database.
ntp.conf	Configuration file for the Network Time Protocol daemon, which synchronizes system time by accessing a remote server.

Table A-2. The /etc directory (continued)

File or directory	Description
openldap/	Directory that contains configuration files for OpenLDAP, an implementation of the Lightweight Directory Access Protocol.
pam.d/	Directory that contains configuration files for PAM .
passwd	Password file. For more information, see Chapter 3.
periodic/	Directory that contains configuration files for the *periodic* utility, which runs *cron* jobs on a regular basis.
ppp/	Contains configuration files for Point-To-Point Tunneling Protocol (PPTP). Mac OS X Server only.
printcap	Printer configuration file for *lpd*. CUPS automatically generates this file. For more information, see *cupsd(8)*.
profile	Global profile for the Bourne-again shell.
protocols	Network protocol database.
racoon/	Directory that contains configuration files for *raccoon*, the IKE key management daemon.
rc	Startup script for multiuser mode.
rc.boot	Startup script for single-user mode.
rc.cleanup	Cleanup script invoked by */etc/rc*.
rc.common	Common settings for startup scripts.
rc.netboot	Startup script for booting from the network using NetBoot.
resolv.conf	DNS resolver configuration.
resolver/	Contains files used to resolve hostnames.
rmtab	Remote NFS mount table.
rpc	RPC number-to-name mappings. Mac OS X 10.1 and earlier consulted this file only in single-user mode, but Mac OS X 10.2 (Jaguar) uses this file at other times. For more information, see Chapter 3.
rtadvd.conf	Configuration file for the router advertisement daemon. For more details, see *rtadvd(8)*.
servermgrd/	Configuration files for the Server Manager daemon. Mac OS X Server only.
services	Internet service name database. Mac OS X 10.1 and earlier consulted this file only in single-user mode, but Mac OS X 10.2 (Jaguar) uses this file at other times. For more information, see Chapter 3.
shells	List of shells.
slpsa.conf	Configuration file for the service locator daemon (*slpd*).
smb.conf	Samba configuration file.
smb.conf.template	Template configuration file for Samba.
squirrelmail/	Configuration files for SquirrelMail, a web-based email client. See *http://www.squirrelmail.org*. Mac OS X Server only.
ssh_config	Global configuration file for OpenSSH client programs.

File or directory	Description
ssh_host_dsa_key	Private DSA host key for OpenSSH. This file, and the other ssh_host_* files, are created the first time you start Remote Login in the Sharing System Preferences.
ssh_host_dsa_key.pub	Public DSA host key for OpenSSH.
ssh_host_key	Private host key for OpenSSH when using SSH 1 compatibility.
ssh_host_key.pub	Public host key for OpenSSH when using SSH 1 compatibility.
ssh_host_rsa_key	Private RSA host key for OpenSSH.
ssh_host_rsa_key.pub	Public RSA host key for OpenSSH.
sshd_config	Configuration file for the OpenSSH sshd daemon.
sudoers	Configuration file for the sudo command. Make sure you use the visudo command only to edit this file.
syslog.conf	syslogd configuration file.
ttys	Terminal initialization file.
ttys.installer	Description not available at time of writing; see errata page at http://www.oreilly.com/catalog/mosxgeeks.
watchdog.conf	Configuration file for Mac OS X Server's watchdog service. Watchdog restarts certain daemons if they die (similar to System V inittab).
webperfcache	File that contains configuration files for Mac OS X Server's webperfcache service, which sits between port 80 and your web server and caches static pages.
weekly	Weekly cron job (see crontab). This is a symlink to /etc/periodic/weekly/500.weekly.
xinetd.conf	Configuration file for xinetd, the extended Internet superserver daemon.
xinetd.d/	File that contains service-specific configuration files for xinetd.
xtab	Description not available at time of writing; see errata page at http://www.oreilly.com/catalog/mosxgeeks.

The /System/Library Directory

Table A-3 lists the directories stored under the */System/Library* directory. You should not modify the contents of these directories or add new files to them. Instead, use their counterparts in the */Library* folder. For example, to install a new font, drag it into */Library/Fonts*, not */System/Library/Fonts*.

Table A-3. The /System/Library directory

File or directory	Description
Axis/	Contains support files for Apache Axis. Mac OS X Server only.
Assistants/	Contains support files for the setup assistant. Mac OS X Server only.
Caches/	Contains caches used by various parts of the operating system.
CFMSupport/	Holds shared libraries used by Carbon applications.
Classic/	Description not available at time of writing; see errata page at http://www.oreilly.com/catalog/mosxgeeks.

File or directory	Description
ColorPickers/	Includes localized resources for Mac OS X color pickers.
Colors/	Lists the names and values of colors used in the color picker control.
ColorSync/	Contains ColorSync profiles.
Components/	Contains application building blocks (components), such as AppleScript and color pickers. Components are not applications themselves and are generally shared between applications.
CoreServices/	Contains system applications, such as *SystemStarter, BootX*, the Finder, and the login window.
Displays/	Contains ColorSync information for external monitors.
DTDs/	Contains document type definitions for XML documents used by the system, such as property lists.
Extensions/	Holds Darwin kernel extensions.
Extensions.kextcache	Contains information about extensions in the cache; a compressed XML document.
Extensions.mkext	Contains the kernel extension cache. It is created at boot by */etc/rc*.
Filesystems/	Contains drivers and utilities for various filesystems (MS-DOS, AppleShare, UFS, etc.).
Find/	Includes support files for Sherlock's content indexing.
Fonts/	Contains core Mac OS X fonts.
Frameworks/	Holds a collection of reusable application frameworks, including shared libraries, headers, and documentation.
Image Capture/	Contains device support files for the Image Capture application.
Java/	Contains Java *class* and *jar* files.
Keyboard Layouts/	Contains bundles that support internationalized keyboard layouts.
Keyboards/	Contains keyboard mappings.
Keychains/	Contains system-wide keychain files. (*~/Library/Keychains* contains per-user keychains.)
LoginPlugins/	Contains helper applications that are launched as you log in.
Modem Scripts/	Contains modem configuration scripts.
MonitorPanels/	Includes panels used by System Preferences → Displays.
OpenSSL/	Holds OpenSSL configuration and support files.
Perl/	Holds Perl Libraries.
PHP/	Contains PHP Libraries.
PreferencePanes/	Contains all the preference panes for the Preferences application.
Printers/	Contains printer support files.
PrivateFrameworks/	Holds private frameworks meant to support Mac OS X. These frameworks are not meant for programmers' use.
QuickTime/	Holds QuickTime support files.
QuickTimeJava/	Includes support files for the QuickTime/Java bridge.

File or directory	Description
Rulebooks/	Contains information used for text handling, such as word-breaking rules for hyphenation.
Screen Savers/	Contains screensavers that you can select from System Preferences → Screen Saver.
ScriptingAdditions/	Includes AppleScript plug-ins and libraries.
Server Settings/	Contains plug-ins for the Server Settings utility. Mac OS X Server only.
ServerSetup/	Contains support files used when setting the initial server configuration. Mac OS X Server only.
Services/	Contains services that are made available through the Services menu.
Sounds/	Contains sounds that are available in System Preferences → Sound.
Speech/	Includes speech recognition and generation support files.
StartupItems/	Contains startup scripts as described in Chapter 2.
SystemConfiguration/	Contains plug-ins used to monitor various system activities (for Apple use only).
SystemResources/	Contains precompiled header lists for the C compiler (see "Precompiled Header Files" in Chapter 5).
Tcl/	Holds *Tcl* libraries.
TextEncodings/	Contains localized text encodings.
User Template/	Lists localized skeleton files for user directories. See "Creating a User's Home Directory" in Chapter 3.

The /Library Directory

Table A-4 lists the contents of the */Library* directory. This directory contains counterparts to many directories found in */System/Library*. You can use the */Library* counterparts for system-wide customization. If you find a directory of the same name in your home *Library* directory (*~/Library*), you can use that for user-level customization. For example, you can install fonts for one particular user by moving them into *~/username/Library/Fonts*.

Table A-4. The /Library directory

File or directory	Description
Application Support/	Contains support files for locally installed applications.
Audio/	Contains audio plug-ins and sounds.
Authenticators/	Contains authentication code for locally installed applications.
Caches/	Contains cached data used by various parts of the operating system.

File or directory	Description
CFMSupport/	Holds shared libraries used by Carbon applications.
ColorSync/	Contains user-installed ColorSync profiles and scripts.
Desktop Pictures/	Contains desktop pictures used by System Preferences → Desktop.
Documentation/	Provides documentation for locally installed applications.
FTPServer/	Contains configuration files and the *root* folder of anonymous FTP server. Mac OS X Server only.
Filesystems/	Contains authentication support for the Apple Share network client.
Fonts/	Contains locally installed fonts.
Image Capture/	Contains locally installed scripts and plug-ins for the Image Capture application.
Internet Plug-Ins/	Contains locally installed browser plug-ins.
Java/	Contains locally installed Java classes (you can drop jar files into */Library/Java/ Extensions*), as well as a suitable directory to use as your $JAVA_HOME (*/Library/Java/ Home*).
Keyboard Layouts/	Contains keyboard mappings.
Logs/	Holds logs for services such as Apple File Services, the Crash Reporter, and the Directory Service.
Macintosh Manager/	Contains support files for the Macintosh Manager application (Mac OS X Server only).
Modem Scripts/	Holds support files for various modem types.
Perl/	Lists locally installed Perl modules (MakeMaker's INSTALLSITELIB).
PreferencePanes/	Contains system preference panes for locally installed utilities such as TinkerTool.
Preferences/	Lists global preferences.
Printers/	Lists printer drivers and utilities.
QuickTime/	Contains locally installed QuickTime components.
QuickTimeStreaming/	Contains the QuickTime Streaming Server (Mac OS X Server only).
Receipts/	Leaves a receipt in the form of a *.pkg* directory after you install an application with the Mac OS X installer. The *.pkg* directory contains a bill of materials file (*.bom*), which you can read with the *lsbom* command.
Screen Savers/	Lists locally installed screensavers.
Scripts/	Contains a variety of AppleScripts installed with Mac OS X.
StartupItems/	Lists locally installed startup items. See "Adding Startup Items" in Chapter 2.
Tomcat/	Holds the Apache Tomcat Java Servlet and JSP server (Mac OS X Server only).
User Pictures/	Contains user pictures that are used in the login panel.
WebServer/	Contains the Apache CGI and document *root* directories.

The /var Directory

The */var* directory contains transient and volatile files, such as PID files (which tell you the process ID of a currently running daemon), log files, and many others. Table A-5 lists the contents of the */var* directory.

Table A-5. The /var directory

File or directory	Description
at/	Contains information about jobs scheduled with the *at* command.
backups/	Contains backups of the NetInfo database.
cron/	Contains user *crontab* files.
db/	Includes a grab bag of configuration and data files, including the *locate* database, the NetInfo database, and network interface information.
empty/	Description not available at time of writing; see errata page at *http://www.oreilly.com/catalog/mosxgeeks*.
log/	Contains a variety of log files, including *syslog*, mail, and web server logs.
mail/	Contains inboxes for local users' email.
msgs/	Holds system-wide messages that were delivered using *msgs -s*.
named/	Includes various files used for local DNS services.
netboot/	Contains various files used for NetBoot.
root/	Serves as the *root* user's home directory.
run/	Holds PID files for running processes. Also contains working files used by programs such as *sudo*.
rwho/	Contains information used by the *rwho* command.
servermgrd/	Contains runtime files used by the Server Manager daemon. Mac OS X Server only.
spool/	Serves as a spool directory for mail, printer queues, and other queued resources.
tmp/	Serves as a temporary file directory.
vm/	Contains your swap files.
yp/	Contains files used by NIS.

The /dev Directory

The */dev* directory contains files that represent devices attached to the system, including physical devices, such as serial ports, and pseudodevices, such as a random number generator. Table A-6 lists the contents of the */dev* directory.

Table A-6. The /dev directory

File or directory	Description
bpf[0-3]	Berkeley Packet Filter devices. See *bpf(4)*.
console	The system console. This is owned by whoever is currently logged in. If you write to it, the output will end up in */var/tmp/console.log*, which you can view with the Console application (*/Applications/Utilities*).
cu.modem	Modem device for compatibility with the Unix *cu* (call up) utility.
disk[0-n]	Disk.
disk[0-n]s[0-n]	Disk partition. For example, */dev/disk0s1* is the first partition of */dev/disk0*.
fd/	Devices that correspond to file descriptors. See the *fd* manpage for more details.
klog	Device used by *syslogd* to read kernel messages.
kmem	Image of kernel memory.
mem	Image of the system memory.
null	Bit bucket. You can redirect anything here, and it will disappear.
ptyp[0-f]	Master ends of the first sixteen pseudo-*ttys*.
pty[q-w][0-f]	Master ends of the remaining pseudo-*ttys*.
random	Source of pseudorandom data. See *random(4)*.
rdisk[0-n]	Raw disk device.
rdisk[0-n]s[0-n]	Raw disk partition.
stderr	Symbolic link to */dev/fd/2*.
stdin	Symbolic link to */dev/fd/0*.
stdout	Symbolic link to */dev/fd/1*.
tty	Standard output stream of the current Terminal or remote login.
tty.modem	Modem device.
ttyp[0-f]	Slave ends of the first sixteen pseudo-*ttys*.
tty[q-w][0-f]	Slave ends of the remaining pseudo-*ttys*.
urandom	Source of pseudorandom data, not guaranteed to be strong. See *random(4)*.
vn[0-3]	Pseudo disk devices.
zero	Infinite supply of null characters. Often used with *dd* to create a file made up of null characters.

Command-Line Tools: The Missing Manpages

Unfortunately, many of the command-line utilities in Mac OS X have no corresponding manpages, and documentation on the utilities can be difficult to find, even with a Google search. This appendix offers a quick reference to tools that may be helpful or interesting to Mac OS X developers, but that lack manpages.

Each of the following sections includes the command syntax, a brief description, the directory location of the command, and the operating system with which it comes. Note that tools released with Darwin are also included in Mac OS X.

aexml

Syntax

```
aexml -soap -SOAPAction text [-in filename] [-out filename] [-name 'App
Name' | -pid pid | psn highPSN.lowPSN | -sig signature]
aexml -xmlrpc [-in filename] [-out filename] [-name 'App Name' | -pid pid |
psn highPSN.lowPSN | -sig signature]
```

Description

Translates SOAP and XML-RPC requests into Apple Events understood by Mac OS X applications. The target application can be specified by name, process ID, process serial number, or signature. If no target is specified, a sandbox application is launched to handle the request. Output, if any, is in the form of XML or a one-line error.

Options/Usage

-soap
    Forwards a SOAP request to the target application.

-SOAPAction
> Provides the SOAPAction header. If specified as -, the header is read from input.

-xmlrpc
> Forwards an XML-RPC request to the target application.

-in Specifies source of input. Defaults to - (standard input).

-out
> Specifies location of output. Defaults to - (standard output).

-name
> Specifies target application by pathname.

-pid
> Specifies target application by Unix PID.

-psn
> Specifies target application by Carbon Process Manager process serial number.

-sig
> Specifies target application by signature. This is a four-character code unique to an application. The signature is usually the same as the application's creator code. In an application bundle, it is specified by the CFBundleSignature property in *Info.plist*.

Location
/usr/bin

Operating System
Mac OS X

---

configd

Syntax
config d [-b] [-B *bundle_ID*] [-d] [-t *pathname*] [-v] [-V *bundle_ID*]

Description
This is the System Configuration Server. *configd* is normally started as a daemon during the boot process. It monitors changes to network-related items, such as link status, DHCP assignments, PPP connections, and IP configuration, and provides an API for applications to be notified of these changes. To monitor various items, it uses a set of plug-in configuration agents, including the Preferences Monitor, the Kernel Event Monitor, the PPP Controller Agent, the IP Configuration Agent, and the IP Monitor Agent. The agent plug-ins are located in */System/Library/SystemConfiguration*.

More information on the System Configuration framework can be found at *http://developer.apple.com/techpubs/macosx/Networking/SysConfigOverview926/*.

Options/Usage

-*b*   Disables loading of all agents.

-*B*   Disables loading of the specified agent.

-*d*   Disables daemonization; runs process in foreground.

-*t*   Loads the agent specified by *pathname*.

-*v*   Enables verbose logging.

-*V*   Enables verbose logging for the specified agent.

Location

/usr/sbin

Operating System

Darwin

DirectoryService

Syntax

```
DirectoryService [-h | -v]
DirectoryService [-appledebug | -appleframework | -applenodaemon | -
appleoptions | -appleperformance | -appleversion]
```

Description

This is the server process for the Directory Services framework.

Options/Usage

-*h*   Prints a usage statement for the first form of command invocation to standard output.

-*v*   Prints software release version to standard output.

-*appledebug*
   Runs service in debug mode.

-*appleframework*
   Starts service normally. This is the default.

-*applenodaemon*
   Disables daemonization; runs service in foreground.

-*appleoptions*
   Prints a usage statement for the second form of command invocation to standard output.

-appleperformance
Runs service in foreground and logs extensively.

-appleversion
Prints software build version to standard output.

Location

/usr/sbin

Operating System

Darwin

---

disktool

Syntax

```
disktool [-o | -r | -x | -y]
disktool [-d | -g | -m | -va | -vd | -vs] device
disktool [-e | -p | -s | -u] device integer_flag
disktool -n device vol_name
disktool -a device vol_name vol_flags
```

Description

Controls disks, including mounting, unmounting, ejecting, enabling permissions, and volume naming. Most options require a device name argument (for example, disk0), and some options require additional parameters.

Options/Usage

-a Adds disk to Disk Arbitration tables, to notify applications of a mounted volume. This is useful if you have forced a mount, thus bypassing standard notification.

-d Removes disk from Disk Arbitration tables, to notify applications of a dismount. This is useful if you have forced a dismount, thus bypassing standard notification.

-e Ejects disk. Takes an additional argument that is normally set to 0.

-g Gets HFS encoding on a volume.

-m Mounts disk.

-n Names volume.

-o Opens vacant drive doors.

-p Unmounts partition. Device name is that of a partition (for example, disk0s5). Takes an additional argument that is normally set to 0.

-r Refreshes Disk Arbitration.

-s Sets HFS encoding on a volume. Takes encoding as additional integer argument.

-u   Unmounts disk. Takes an additional argument that is normally set to 0.

-va Adds device to */var/db/volinfo.database*.

-vd Deletes device from */var/db/volinfo.database*.

-vs Displays status of device in */var/db/volinfo.database*.

-x   Disallows dismounts and ejects.

-y   Allows dismounts and ejects.

Location

/usr/sbin

Operating System

Darwin

---

dynamic_pager

Syntax

```
dynamic_pager [-F filename] [-H hire_point]  [-L layoff_point] [-P priority]
[-S file_size]
```

Description

Manages virtual memory swap files. This tool is started from */etc/rc* during the boot process.

Options/Usage

-F   Specifies the base absolute pathname for swap files. Swap filenames consist of this base and a whole number suffix, starting at 0. The default is */private/var/vm/swapfile*.

-H   Creates an additional swap file when free swap space drops below the *hire_point* in bytes. The default is 0, which disables the use of this swap space.

-L   Attempts to consolidate memory and remove a swap file when free swap space rises above the *layoff_point* in bytes. The *layoff_point* must be set higher than the sum of the swap file size and the *hire_point*, unless it is set to 0 (the default), which disables layoffs.

-P   Determines the priority of this swap space. The default is 0.

-S   Determines the size of swap files created, in bytes. The default is 20000000.

Location

/sbin

Operating System

Darwin

---

ipconfig

Syntax

```
ipconfig getifaddr interface
ipconfig getoption { interface | "" } { option_name | option_code }
ipconfig getpacket interface
ipconfig ifcount
ipconfig set interface { BOOTP | DHCP }
ipconfig set interface { INFORM | MANUAL } IP_addr netmask
ipconfig waitall
```

Description

Interacts with the IP Configuration Agent of *configd* to manage network configuration changes.

Options/Usage

getifaddr
Prints the specified network interface's IP address to standard output.

getoption
Prints the value of the specified DHCP option to standard output. If *interface* is specified, the option is interface-specific. If empty quotes are used instead, the option is global. Option names and numeric codes are DHCP-standard (such as host_name, domain_name, netinfo_server_address, etc.).

getpacket
Prints DHCP transaction packets to standard output.

ifcount
Prints the number of network interfaces to standard output.

set
Sets the method by which the specified network interface is assigned an IP address. Using *BOOTP* or *DHCP* causes the system to attempt to contact a server of the appropriate type to obtain IP configuration information. Using *INFORM* sets the IP address locally, but initiates a DHCP request to obtain additional IP configuration information (DNS servers, default gateway, etc.). Using *MANUAL* indicates that all IP configuration information is set locally.

waitall
Sets the configurations of all network interfaces according to the specifications in */etc/iftab*.

Location

/usr/sbin

Operating System

Darwin

opendiff

Syntax

```
opendiff file1 file2 [-ancestor ancestor_file] [-merge merge_file]
```

Description

Opens the two designated files in the FileMerge application.

Options/Usage

-ancestor
> Compares the two files against a common ancestor file.

-merge
> Merges the two files into a new file.

Location

> */usr/bin*

Operating System

> Mac OS X

---

pbcopy

Syntax

```
pbcopy [-help]
```

Description

Copies standard input to the pasteboard buffer. The pasteboard is used to implement GUI copy, cut, and paste operations, drag-and-drop operations, and the Cocoa Services menu.

Options/Usage

-help
> Prints an unhelpful usage statement to standard output.

Location

> */usr/bin*

Operating System

> Mac OS X

---

pbpaste

Syntax

```
pbpaste[-help] [-Prefer { ascii | rtf | ps }]
```

Description

Prints the contents of the pasteboard to standard output. The combination of *pbcopy* and *pbpaste* may be an interesting tool to use in scripting. However, the system's global pasteboard can be modified by other processes at any time, which limits the tool's actual usefulness.

Options/Usage

-help
> Prints a usage statement to standard output.

-Prefer
> Specifies the output format to use if the desired format (ASCII, Rich Text Format, or PostScript) is available in the pasteboard.

Location

> */usr/bin*

Operating System

> Mac OS X

---

pl

Syntax

```
pl [-input input_binary_file | -output output_binary_file]
```

Description

Translates XML property list files into a more compact "key = value" format. Also translates between this and a serialized binary format, in either direction. XML is read from standard input, "key = value" data is read from standard input and written to standard output, and serialized binary data is read from and written to files specified with arguments.

Options/Usage

-input
> Specifies a serialized binary file as input.

-output
> Specifies a serialized binary file as output.

Examples

cat *foo.plist* | **pl**
> Translates XML property list to "key = value" format.

cat *foo.plist* | **pl** | **pl -output** *foo.bin*
> Translates XML property list to serialized binary format.

pl -input *foo.bin*
> Translates serialized binary file to "key = value" format.

Location

> */usr/bin*

Operating System

> Mac OS X

---

scselect

Syntax

> scselect [[-n] *location*]

Description

Changes active network *location*, similar to selecting a network Location from the Apple menu. If there are no arguments, a usage statement and a list of defined Locations (or "sets") as defined in the Network System Preferences panel is printed to standard output, along with an indication of which location is currently active. Locations can be referred to by name or by integer ID.

Options/Usage

-n Changes the active network Location, but does not apply the change.

Location

> */usr/sbin*

Operating System

> Darwin

scutil

Syntax

```
scutil [-r node_or_address | -w key [-t timeout]]
```

Description

Provides control of the System Configuration framework's dynamic store. *scutil* opens an interactive session with *configd*, in which various commands are available to view and modify System Configuration keys.

As a quick sample run-through, invoke *scutil*. You will be placed at the *scutil* prompt. Enter *open* to start the session with *configd*, then enter *list*. You will see a set of keys, some of which are provided by the System Configuration framework (such as the keys in the File: domain), some of which are obtained from the preferences file */var/db/SystemConfiguration.xml* (the Setup: keys), and some of which are published by the configuration agents (the State: keys). Enter **get State:/ Network/Global/DNS** to load the dictionary associated with that key. Then run *d. show* to display it. You should see a list of DNS servers and search domains configured on your system. Finally, run *close*, then *quit*.

Options/Usage

-r   Checks for reachability of the node or address. (Any numerical argument seems to result in Reachable status.)

-t   Specifies the timeout to wait for the presence of a data store key, in seconds. The default is 15.

-w   Exits when the specified key exists in the data store or when the timeout has expired.

Commands

scutil enters interactive mode when it is invoked with no arguments.

add key [temporary]
> Adds a key to the data store with the value of the current dictionary. The temporary keyword causes it to be flushed when the session to *configd* is closed.

close
> Closes a session with *configd*.

d.add key [* | ? | #] value...
> Adds an entry to the current dictionary. The optional type specifier can designate the values as arrays (*****), booleans (**?**), or numbers (**#**).

d.init
> Creates an empty dictionary.

d.remove key
> Removes the specified key from the current dictionary.

d.show
> Displays the contents of the current dictionary.

f.read file
> Reads prepared commands from a file.

get key
> Causes the value of the specified key to become the current dictionary.

help
> Prints a list of available commands.

list [key_pattern]
> Lists keys in the System Configuration data store. The *key_pattern* can restrict which keys are output, but *key_pattern* appears to be quite limited.

n.add { key | key_pattern }
> Requests notification of changes to the specified keys.

n.cancel
> Cancels *n.watch* settings.

n.changes
> Lists changed keys that have been marked with notification requests.

n.list [key_pattern]
> Lists keys upon which notification requests have been set.

n.remove { key | key_pattern }
> Removes notification requests for the specified keys.

n.watch [verbose]
> Causes changes to keys marked with notification requests to issue immediate notices, obviating the need to use *n.changes* to serve notice that the change has occurred.

notify key
> Sends a notification for the specified key.

open
> Opens a session with *configd*.

quit
> Exits the *scutil* session.

remove key
> Removes the specified key from the data store.

set key
> Sets the specified key to the value of the current dictionary.

Location

/usr/sbin

Operating System

Darwin

SplitForks

Syntax

SplitForks { -u | [-v] *pathname* }

Description

Splits the resource fork out of a dual-forked file into a file named .*_pathname*. You can also do this with **cp** *pathname***/..namedfork/rsrc** .*_pathname*. This method results in a resource file amenable to processing by *DeRez*, whereas the output of *SplitForks* does not appear to produce a file that *DeRez* can understand.

Options/Usage

-u   Prints a usage statement to standard output.

-v   Enables verbose output.

Location

/Developer/Tools

Operating System

Mac OS X

tiff2icns

Syntax

tiff2icns [-noLarge] *input_filename* [*output_filename*]

Description

Converts TIFF image files to Apple icon (ICNS) files. If *output_filename* is not specified, the output file receives the same name as the input file, with the file-name extension changed to *.icns*.

Options/Usage

-noLarge
Prevents the creation of the highest resolution icons.

Location

/usr/bin

Operating System

Mac OS X

---

tiffutil

Syntax

```
tiffutil { -dump | -info | -verboseinfo } input_file…
tiffutil { -extract number | -jpeg [-fN] | -lzw | -none | -packbits }
input_file [-out output_file]
tiffutil -cat input_file… [-out output_file]
```

Description

Manipulates TIFF image files.

Options/Usage

-cat
Concatenates multiple input files.

-dump
Prints a list of all tags in the input file to standard output.

-extract
Extracts an individual image from the input file, with 0 designating the first image in the file.

-f

Specifies the compression factor to use with JPEG compression. The value can range from 1 to 255. The default is 10.

-info
Prints information about images in the input file to standard output.

-jpeg
Specifies the use of JPEG compression when producing the output file.

-lzw
Specifies the use of Lempel-Ziv-Welch compression when producing the output file.

-none
Specifies the use of no compression when producing the output file.

-output
> Specifies the name of the output file; defaults to *out.tiff*.

-packbits
> Specifies the use of PackBits compression when producing the output file.

-verboseinfo
> Prints lots of information about images in the input file to standard output.

Location

> */usr/bin*

Operating System

> Mac OS X

---

udf.util

Syntax

```
udf.util -m device mount_point
udf.util { -p | -u } device
```

Description

Mounts UDF (DVD) filesystems into the directory hierarchy.

Options/Usage

-m Mounts the device.

-p Probes the device for mounting.

-u Unmounts the device.

device
> Specifies the DVD device filename, for example, **disk1**.

mount_point
> Specifies the directory on which the DVD filesystem will be mounted.

Location

> */System/Library/Filesystems/udf.fs*

Operating System

> Darwin

vsdbutil

Syntax

```
vsdbutil { -a | -c | -d } pathname
vsdbutil -i
```

Description

Enables or disables the use of permissions on a disk volume. This is equivalent to using the Ignore Privileges checkbox in the Finder's Info window for a mounted volume. The status of permissions usage on mounted volumes is stored in the permissions database, */var/db/volinfo.database*.

Options/Usage

-a   Activates permissions on the volume designated by *pathname*.

-c   Checks the status of permissions usage on the volume designated by *pathname*.

-d   Deactivates permissions on the volume designated by *pathname*.

-i   Initializes the permissions database to include all mounted HFS and HFS+ volumes.

Location

/usr/sbin

Operating System

Darwin

Index

We'd like to hear your suggestions for improving our indexes. Send email to *index@oreilly.com*.

BootX loader, 32
Bourne shell, 3
BSD, 32
    configuration files for, 45
    flat files and, 46
build type, 71
BuildStrings tool, 23
-bundle option, 85
bundles, 85
    loading dynamically, 87–88
bytes, endian order of, 76

C

C compiler, 67, 69
C pointers, size of, 76
calculator, dc command for, 31
Carnegie Mellon University, Mach
    developed by, 32
cat command, 28
cc command, 23, 73
cc compiler, 69
    special flags for, 85
cd command, 28
characters, positioning commands for
    (vi mode), 18
chflags command, 28
chmod command, 28
clear command, 31
click to position cursor option, 9
clipboard, Terminal and, 4
cmp command, 28
code (see source code; sample code)
comm command, 28
.command files, 6
command line, 3–31
    creating disk images from, 118
    downloading files from, 14
    editing from, with tcsh shell, 15–19
    history commands for
        Emacs mode, 16
        vi mode, 17
command-line switches, 3
command-line utilities, 23, 174–188
command prompt, 4
command submode (vi mode), 17
commands, 15–31
    information about, man command
        for, 31
    via keystrokes, 16–19

locating by keyword, apropos
    command for, 31
Compiler Tools, 68
compilers, 67, 69
compiling source code, 67–77
    steps in, 70
compress tool, 30
configd command, 175
configuration files in /etc
    directory, 165–168
configure scripts, 70–72
console messages, displaying during
    startup, 32
context switches, latency utility for
    measuring, 132
cp command, 28
cpio tool, 30
cplutil tool, 23
CpMac tool, 23
cpp (GNU C preprocessor), 74
    caution with, 81
cpp-precomp (precompilation
    preprocessor), 74
    caution with, 81
    vs. PFE mechanism, 82
creating
    hosts, 60
    packages, 101–104
    static libraries, 91
    Terminals, 5–10
    user properties, 59
    users, 58
cron jobs, 41
.cshrc file, caution in presence of .tcshrc
    file, 12
curl utility, 101
curses screen library, 84
cursor
    click to position option for, 9
    editing commands for (vi mode), 17
    positioning commands for (Emacs
        mode), 16
cut tool, 26
CVS archive, obtaining/using source
    code from, 125
CVS tags, 127
cvs tool, 22
CVSWeb archive (Darwin), 127
cvs-wrap/cvs-unwrap tools, 23

P

.p file extension, 78
PackageMaker tool, 105, 106–111
packages
    creating/installing, 101–104
        using PackageMaker
            for, 106–111
        /usr/local directory for, 113
    disadvantages of tarballs for
        distributing, 113
packaging tools, 105–119
page faults, sc_usage utility for
    displaying, 133
PAM API, 44
passwords, 44
    changing, passwd command for, 31
    managing, 57–60
paste tool, 26
patch command, 29
pbcopy command, 25, 180
pbhelpindexer tool, 24
pbpaste command, 25, 181
pbprojectdump tool, 24
pbxcp tool, 24
pbxhmapdump tool, 24
perl command, 27
Persistent Front End (PFE)
    mechanism, 82
Persson, Per, 154
PFE precompilation, 82
Pfisterer, Christoph, 96
PGPLOT graph-drawing package, 154
PIC flags, 85
pico tool, 26
pl command, 181
plists (property lists), 141
    for startup items, 39
PORT/PORTING file, 70, 71
ports system, 104
position-independent code (PIC)
    flags, 85
prebinding, 91
precompilation preprocessor (see
    cpp-precomp)
precompiled header files, 78, 80
Preferences pane, 142
preprocessing, 73
printers, cplutil tool for configuring, 23
printf command, 27

process information, top utility for
    displaying, 130–132
programming, Directory Services
    and, 43
programming languages, GCC support
    for, 73
Project Athena, 12
Project Builder, 68
    tools for, 23, 24
prompts, 49
property lists (plists), 141
    for startup items, 39
protocols, 44–63
proto.term, 6
pwd command, 29

Q

Quartz/Quartz Extreme, 146
quoting file/directory names, 14

R

ranlib command, 91
rc scripts, 33
rcp command, 29
rcs command, 23
RCS, cvs tool and, 22
README file, 70, 71
Red Hat, 96
Rendezvous protocol, 46
ResMerger tool, 24
resource files, tools for, 24
resource forks, commands/tools for, 23,
    24
resource strings, BuildStrings tool
    for, 23
resources for further reading, xii
    assembler and PowerPC machine
        language, 77
    Developer Tools, 67
    flat file formats, 61
    kernel extension tutorials, 136
    Mac OS X, x
    NetInfo utilities, 50
    PAM API, 44
    prebinding, 91
    precompiled header files, 81
Rez tool, 24
RezWack tool, 24
rm/rmdir commands, 29

About the Authors

Brian Jepson is a "100-foot-tall nonstudent" who specialized in social sabotage as a student at the University of Rhode Island. His on-again, off-again coffeehouse, Cafe de la Tete, was part of a successful "culture jamming" experiment disguised as a program for mass liberation. Not content to enjoy the relaxed life of a coffeehouse operator and student, Brian made his way to Wall Street, where he remained cleverly disguised as a database programmer for many years. As he grew older and wiser, he worked more and more with free software and encourages others to do the same. Brian has written several books, including *Database Application Programming with Linux* (John Wiley & Sons) and the *Perl Resource Kit Utilities Guide* (O'Reilly). He is now a writer for O'Reilly & Associates, Inc. He keeps a watchful gaze on many corners of technology, including web services, .NET, Mac OS X, portable computing, and wireless networking. You can follow his movements at *http://www.jepstone.net*.

Ernest E. Rothman is an associate professor of mathematics at Salve Regina University (SRU), where he is also chair of the mathematical sciences department, as well as manager of the computational science program. Before SRU, Ernie held the position of research associate at the Cornell Theory Center at Cornell University. Ernie holds a Ph.D. in applied mathematics from Brown University. His academic interests are primarily in scientific computing and computational science education. Ernie also enjoys playing with Linux systems, including Solaris, Linux, and Mac OS X.

Colophon

Our look is the result of reader comments, our own experimentation, and feedback from distribution channels. Distinctive covers complement our distinctive approach to technical topics, breathing personality and life into potentially dry subjects.

The animal on the cover of *Mac OS X for Unix Geeks* is a foxhound. The foxhound's coat is short, hard, and glossy and can be black, tan, white, or a combination of these colors. Foxhounds are generally free of many of the heritable defects that afflict other large dog breeds. They usually stand 21 to 27 inches tall at the shoulder, and their average weight is 55 to 75 pounds.

The English foxhound traces its ancestry back to the 1600s. Foxhounds were bred specifically to hunt foxes, so they require great stamina, strength, and speed. They are known for their superior scenting powers and strong, melodious voices. Amerian foxhounds, developed from stock brought over from England in the 1650s, are hardier and finer-boned than their English counterparts. They were bred to adapt to more rugged terrain, where they hunted foxes, coyotes, and deer.

Foxhounds are friendly, intelligent, courageous pack hounds with a cheerful, determined disposition. They tend to be easygoing and affectionate, and although they can be strong-willed, they are not aggressive. Foxhounds were bred mainly as hunting dogs, rather than as family pets. They are a very active breed, requiring lots of exercise, and they tend to be happiest with owners who live in rural areas or on large farms. Foxhounds enjoy the company of other dogs and can become bored if kept alone.

Claire Cloutier was the production editor and copyeditor for *Mac OS X for Unix Geeks*. Ann Schirmer was the proofreader. Ann Schirmer, Linley Dolby, and Jeffrey Holcomb provided quality control. Claire Cloutier, Kimo Carter, and Genevieve d'Entremont were the compositors. Brenda Miller wrote the index.

Emma Colby designed the cover of this book, based on a series design by Edie Freedman. The cover image is a 19th-century engraving from the *Royal Natural History*. Emma Colby produced the cover layout with QuarkXPress 4.1, using Adobe's ITC Garamond font.

David Futato designed the interior layout. This book was converted to FrameMaker 5.5.6 with a format conversion tool created by Erik Ray, Jason McIntosh, Neil Walls, and Mike Sierra that uses Perl and XML technologies. The text font is Linotype Birka; the heading font is Adobe Myriad Condensed; and the code font is LucasFont's TheSans Mono Condensed. The illustrations that appear in the book were produced by Robert Romano and Jessamyn Read using Macromedia FreeHand 9 and Adobe Photoshop 6. The tip and warning icons were drawn by Christopher Bing. This colophon was written by Rachel Wheeler.

Other Titles Available from O'Reilly

Macintosh Users

Mac OS X: The Missing Manual, 2nd Edition

By David Pogue
2nd Edition October 2002
728 pages, ISBN 0-596-00450-8

David Pogue applies his scrupulous objectivity to this exciting new operating system, revealing which new features work well and which do not. This second edition offers a wealth of detail on the myriad changes in OS X 10.2. With new chapters on iChat (Apple's new instant-messaging software), Sherlock 3 (the Web search tool that pulls Web information directly onto the desktop), and the new Finder (which reintroduces spring-loaded folders).

Office X for Macintosh: The Missing Manual

By Nan Barber, Tonya Engst &
David Reynolds
1st Edition July 2002
728 pages, ISBN 0-596-00332-3

This book applies the urbane and readable Missing Manuals touch to a winning topic: Microsoft Office X for Apple's stunning new operating system, Mac OS X. In typical Missing Manual style, targeted sidebars ensure that the book's three sections impart business-level details on Word, Excel, and the Palm-syncable Entourage, without leaving beginners behind. Indispensable reference for a growing user base.

iPhoto: The Missing Manual

By David Pogue, Joseph Schorr &
Derrick Story
1st Edition July 2002
350 pages, ISBN 0-596-00365-x

With this guide, Macintosh fans can take their digital photos to the screen, to the Web, to printouts, to hardbound photo books, even to DVDs. And they'll learn how to take iPhoto far beyond its seemingly simple feature list. But the software is just the beginning. The book also covers choosing and mastering a digital camera, basic photographic techniques, and tips for shooting special subjects like kids, sports, nighttime shots, portraits, and more.

Macintosh Troubleshooting Pocket Guide

By David Lerner & Aaron
Freimark, Tekserve Corporation
1st Edition November 2002 (est.)
80 pages (est.), ISBN 0-596-00443-5

Tekserve Corporation, the distinctive Macintosh repair store in New York City, has long provided its customers with a free "Frequently Asked Questions" document to cover the most common troubleshooting questions. We recently discovered this FAQ sheet and realized that—like New York itself—it was too good to leave just for the New Yorkers. With the help of Tekserve's owners, we turned this FAQ sheet into the *Macintosh Troubleshooting Pocket Guide*.

iMovie 2: The Missing Manual

By David Pogue
1st Edition January 2001
420 pages, ISBN 0-596-00104-5

iMovie 2: The Missing Manual covers every step of iMovie video production, from choosing and using a digital camcorder to burning the finished work onto CDs. Far deeper and more detailed than the meager set of online help screens included with iMovie, the book helps iMovie 2 users realize the software's potential as a breakthrough in overcoming the cost, complexity, and difficulty of desktop video production.

AppleScript in a Nutshell

By Bruce W. Perry
1st Edition June 2001
528 pages, ISBN 1-56592-841-5

AppleScript in a Nutshell is the first complete reference to AppleScript, the popular programming language that gives both power users and sophisticated enterprise customers the important ability to automate repetitive tasks and customize applications. *AppleScript in a Nutshell* is a high-end handbook at a low-end price—an essential desktop reference that puts the full power of this user-friendly programming language into every AppleScript user's hands.

Macintosh Developers

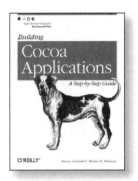  

How to stay in touch with O'Reilly

1. Visit our award-winning web site

http://www.oreilly.com/

★ "Top 100 Sites on the Web"—PC Magazine
★ CIO Magazine's Web Business 50 Awards

Our web site contains a library of comprehensive product information (including book excerpts and tables of contents), downloadable software, background articles, interviews with technology leaders, links to relevant sites, book cover art, and more. File us in your bookmarks or favorites!

2. Join our email mailing lists

Sign up to get email announcements of new books and conferences, special offers, and O'Reilly Network technology newsletters at:

http://elists.oreilly.com

It's easy to customize your free elists subscription so you'll get exactly the O'Reilly news you want.

3. Get examples from our books

To find example files for a book, go to:

http://www.oreilly.com/catalog

select the book, and follow the "Examples" link.

4. Work with us

Check out our web site for current employment opportunites:

http://jobs.oreilly.com/

5. Register your book

Register your book at:
http://register.oreilly.com

6. Contact us

O'Reilly & Associates, Inc.
1005 Gravenstein Hwy North
Sebastopol, CA 95472 USA
TEL: 707-827-7000 or 800-998-9938
     (6am to 5pm PST)
FAX: 707-829-0104

order@oreilly.com
For answers to problems regarding your order or our products. To place a book order online visit:

http://www.oreilly.com/order_new/

catalog@oreilly.com
To request a copy of our latest catalog.

booktech@oreilly.com
For book content technical questions or corrections.

corporate@oreilly.com
For educational, library, government, and corporate sales.

proposals@oreilly.com
To submit new book proposals to our editors and product managers.

international@oreilly.com
For information about our international distributors or translation queries. For a list of our distributors outside of North America check out:

http://international.oreilly.com/distributors.html

adoption@oreilly.com
For information about academic use of O'Reilly books, visit:

http://academic.oreilly.com